V&R unipress

Romantik
Journal for the Study of Romanticisms

Romanti*k*
Journal for the Study of Romanticisms

Volume 12|2023

V&R unipress

Contents

Introduction

The last three issues of Romanti*k* have explored the different ways in which the historical period of romanticism continues to manifest in later times. This is evident in national romanticism which emphasizes a deep emotional connection to one's nation, often rooted in a shared heritage, language, and culture. In the modern era, this sentiment plays a significant role across various facets of culture, albeit in evolved forms still found in the core of e. g., modern literature and even modern art.

In today's globalized world, media and entertainment are powerful vehicles for romantic notions and even romantic nationalism. Movies, television shows, and music often celebrate national identity and heritage, fostering a sense of pride and unity. Films, like *Braveheart* and *The Last of the Mohicans,* blend historical narratives, evoking a romanticized vision of the past. National anthems and patriotic songs remain staples in modern culture as well as football, and the Olympics showcase these anthems, stirring national pride. Additionally, folk and country music often emphasize home, land, and heritage themes, appealing to a romantic sense of nationalism.

Romantic sentiments are still used and frequently surface in political rhetoric and social movements, where they serve as a rallying point for collective identity and action. Politicians emphasize national unity and common heritage. Slogans like "Make America Great Again" leverage emotional connections to national identity. The Catalan independence movement in Spain, and the Scottish independence movement in the UK, are deeply rooted in romantic sentiments. These movements draw on historical narratives and cultural uniqueness to advocate for autonomy.

Art and literature continue to be profound expressions of romantic nationalism, often exploring national identity, heritage, and landscape themes. Modern literature frequently explores national identity through the lens of history and personal narrative. Sports remain one of the most visible arenas for romantic nationalism, providing a stage for celebrating national identity and collective pride.

Romanticism continues to be a potent force in modern culture, evolving to meet the contexts of today's world while retaining its core emotional appeal. From media and politics to art and digital culture, the sense of shared heritage and national pride remains a powerful influence, shaping identities and communities across the globe. As we navigate the complexities of globalization, romanticism offers a way to connect with our roots and fosters a sense of belonging in an increasingly interconnected world.

In the 12th issue of *Romantik*, we will continue the trend of exploring romanticism as a historical epoch and a thought structure which still has an impact onhow we think even in the 21st century. Two articles concentrate on 19th century expressions of romanticism, and three articles explore the different ways in which romantic ideas are reactualized in the late 20th and 21st century.

In his richly illustrated article "Danish Golden Age Painting in a Sentimental Light: Pictures of Childhood", Kasper Lægring employs a new angle on the paintings of the period, from approx. 1801–1864 by focusing on sentimental portrayals of children by e. g., Jens Juel, Constantin Hansen, Wilhelm Marstrand, and lesser known painters, Lægring traces the concept of sentimentality to Jean-Baptiste Greuze. Theoretically, Lægring draws upon Michael Fried's conceptual polarity between absorption and theatricality and Wolfgang Kemp's aesthetics of reception.

In her article, "Figures of Emancipation: Organicist Imagery between Romanticism and Darwinism", Anna Bohlin draws attention to Nordic emancipation novels of the 1850s. By analyzing Collett's *Amtmandens Døttre* (1854–1855), Fibiger's *Clara Raphael* (1851), Bremer's *Hertha* (1856), and Runeberg's *Fru Catharina Boije och hennes döttrar* (1858), Bohlin is able to demonstrate how romantic organicist metaphors legitimize women's emancipation. Additionally, Bohlin traces the change taking place in Collett's essays from the 1870s where organicist imagery is associated with evolutionary biology.

Alda Björk Valdimarsdóttir explores the contemporary reception of Jane Austen in the article: ""The really accomplished young woman, which she wanted to be thought herself." Jane Austen, the chick lit genre, self-help culture, and 18th-century conduct books ". Jane Austen has had a considerable impact on modern chick lit and one can also use the main features of the chick-lit genre to read Austen's stories. Valdimarsdóttir detects a common interest in flawed heroines in Austen and modern chick lit. She argues that "Austen engages in a purposeful dialogue with contemporary conduct books in her novels, just like modern chick lit authors converse with glossy magazines".

In the article, "Oscillating to Decipher the World – On the Timeless Relevance of Early Romantic Irony", Sanna Schulte finds interesting parallels between early romantic Irony and postmodernism. However, the poetological ideas related to early romantic irony are– according to Schulte – both relevant to precursors of romanticism such as Cervantes, but also to postmodern authors such as Italo Calvino: The common thread is self- and meta-reflexive moments leading to a discussion of the precondition for artistic creation. Here, we find the reason for the fascination with romantic aesthetics: It conveys a continuous sense of creation.

Jacob Ølgaard Nyboe also establishes parallels between romanticism and contemporary literature. In the article "Let the Horses Sing and the Astral Lava Flow. On Homosexuality as Transcending Force in Bjørn Rasmussen's *Huden er det elastiske hylster der omgiver hele legemet* and Henrik Bjelke's *Saturn*", Nyboe demonstrates how both novels – written in 2011 and 1974 respectively – are highly influenced by romantic ideas of unification and share a yearning for re-enchantment through sexual epiphany. Concerning both composition and style, Nyboe examines how both novels apply openness, playfulness, and disregard of conventional rules as a means of transgression.

The diversity of the reception of romanticism which these five articles demonstrate, highlights the importance of continuing to explore both historical romanticism and more contemporary forms of romantic thought.

Welcome to the 12th issue of Romanti*k*.

Gísli Magnússon and Kim Simonsen,
on behalf of the editorial board

Kasper Lægring
(University of Aarhus)

Danish Golden Age Painting in a Sentimental Light: Pictures of Childhood[1]

Abstract

This article contributes to the revising and expanding of the concept of the Danish Golden Age by examining sentimentality in late Golden Age paintings of children. First, it delves into the concept of sentimentality in painting, focusing on Jean-Baptiste Greuze (1725–1805), whose art heralds the sentimental. Children's portraits from the early Golden Age by Jens Juel (1745–1802), Constantin Hansen (1804–1880), and Wilhelm Marstrand (1810–1873) serve as a basis for the article's reception-aesthetic examination of sentimental child depictions in the late Golden Age by Peter Julius Larsen (1818–1852), Sophus Schack (1811–1864), and Christian Andreas Schleisner (1810–1882). Elisabeth Jerichau Baumann (1818–1881) is also included. Seventeenth-century Dutch Golden Age painting serves as an additional point of reference. The article concludes that the statuesque posture, low activity level, and placelessness in the image affect the perception of sentimentality, as does the theatrical mode of address (Michael Fried's concept).

Keywords

sentimentality; genre painting; Danish Golden Age; emotions; paintings of children

1 I am indebted to the anonymous reviewer for a number of helpful comments and suggestions for improvement, just as I am to Gísli Magnússon, the editor, for allowing extra time, and thus enabling more plentiful and better illustrations. Also, I extend my sincere thanks to Dr. Jerzy Miskowiak, who has kindly provided me with two of the illustrations of paintings by Elisabeth Jerichau Baumann. I also extend my gratitude to photographer Berit Møller, The Royal Danish Collection, as well as to the following museums for having provided digital image files and waived reproduction fees: Birmingham Museums Trust, Clark Art Institute, The Danish Royal Family, The Nivaagaard Collection, Saint Louis Art Museum, The National Gallery of Denmark, Thorvaldsen's Museum, and Torre Abbey Museum.

Introduction

The task of this article is to flesh out how and when sentimentality emerges in Danish Golden Age painting (approx. 1801–1864), with a particular emphasis on genre and portrait paintings of children.[2] In line with art historian Charlotte Christensen's recent revision of the concept of the Golden Age, which seeks to bring the focus of art history into alignment with what was actually created, bought, and sold during the period, I will call attention to both the overlooked genre of genre painting and some of its Danish practitioners.[3] In determining when sentimentality appears in painting, the works of Jean-Baptiste Greuze (1725–1805) serve as a frame of reference and a starting point for further discussion due to their overt introduction of sentimentality into painting and to their massive impact on the genre of genre painting. My selection of Danish works has been chosen for their representativeness, oscillating between well-known and lesser-known genre painters.

While the literature of the Golden Age was sometimes subject to contemporaneous discussions of sentimentality, similar discussions in the Danish art criticism of the period are few and far between. Since the contemporary reception history of sentimental painting, such as art criticism, diaries, and essays, is thus not abundant enough to form an independent basis for discussion, I have instead drawn upon relevant reception-aesthetic approaches to images.

In any case, these potential written sources could not have stood alone. As Nicola Bown points out in her study of sentimental painting in the Victorian era, we cannot solely rely on a review of textual sources if we want certainty about what could be felt at that time. We must also take the works themselves at face value.[4]

---

2 In recent years, the concept of the 'Danish Golden Age' has been revisited in various ways. The most recent major exhibition dedicated entirely to the Golden Age was the *Danish Golden Age – World-class art between disasters* at the National Gallery of Denmark in 2019. In this exhibition, the time frame of the period was significantly extended, concluding not around 1848, the year of the beginning of the First Schleswig War, but instead with another war year, namely 1864. Similarly, 1801, the year marking the outset of the English Wars, was established as the definitive starting point for the Golden Age. At the same time, new names and new themes were incorporated into the concept of the Golden Age, and overlooked female artists gained greater attention in the exhibition. Peter Nørgaard Larsen and Magnus Olausson, "World art between disasters," in *Danish Golden Age – World class-art between disasters*, ed. Cecilie Høgsbro Østergaard (Copenhagen: The National Gallery of Denmark, 2019).

3 Charlotte Christensen, *Guldalderens billedverden* (Copenhagen: Gyldendal, 2019), 9–15.

4 Nicola Bown, "Tender Beauty: Victorian Painting and the Problem of Sentimentality", *Journal of Victorian Culture* 16, no. 2 (2011): 218. https://doi.org/10.1080/13555502.2011.589678.

Sentimentality as a Concept

Philosopher Marcia Muelder Eaton traces the earliest use of the word 'sentimental' back to 1749 in England. However, it took just one generation for the adjective to deteriorate into a negative label, happening at least as early as 1785.[5]

Her delineation of 'sentimentality' primarily takes a literary path. Philosophers, including Eaton herself, generally believe that sentimentality constitutes a poor attitude towards one's surroundings.[6] But on what grounds? Sentimentality is not a feeling in itself but a mode that can adopt and colour a spectrum of emotions. Through the analysis of a series of predecessors' observations, Eaton arrives at the following definition:

> 'A sentimental mode of thought is typically one that idealizes its object under the guidance of a desire for gratification and reassurance.' Sentimental art works will either display or evoke such modes of thought. For example, they will display inflated language, vague cliches, stock metaphors, etc.[7]

She supplements this with an account of characteristics of both the ethical and aesthetic aspects of sentimentality. Interestingly, these characteristics show that aesthetic judgements fall short even when it comes to evaluating an artwork that is not primarily created for ethical considerations. In other words, it is not a sufficient justification to label something as sentimental simply because exaggerations, clichés, banalities, and worn-out metaphors are employed. Many books, musical pieces, and paintings employ these devices, but far from all are sentimental.[8] As Eaton suggests from the outset, sentimentality relies on an 'inconsistency of thought and action'.[9] In what follows, I will try to trace this discrepancy in compositional terms in order to qualify the notion of sentimentality on art-historical terms. As we shall see, the notion of 'action' will be key to my inquiry.

The essence of sentimentality is self-deception because the obvious and socially expected emotion in a given situation is shifted and diluted into another, less existential surrogate. This dishonesty can only be identified and judged when dealing with either a real social event or an artwork with a realistic character (such as genre painting). Sentimentality becomes apparent when measured against reality and its interpersonal norms and habits, and escapism, in the form of an extreme idealization of the situation or object, therefore plays a central role.

5 Marcia Muelder Eaton, "Laughing at the Death of Little Nell: Sentimental Art and Sentimental People", *American Philosophical Quarterly* 26, no. 4 (1989): 270.
6 Eaton, "Laughing at the Death of Little Nell", 271.
7 Eaton, "Laughing at the Death of Little Nell", 273.
8 Eaton, "Laughing at the Death of Little Nell", 276.
9 Eaton, "Laughing at the Death of Little Nell", 271.

When Oscar Wilde was not convinced by Nelly's character in Charles Dickens' *The Old Curiosity Shop* (1840–41), it was not because the depiction of the kind-hearted girl's death is false but because it is 'shallow or insincere or dishonest'. Similarly, sentimentality involves a degree of bad acting, which is why melodrama is often identified with the sentimental.[10] Eaton's opening statement takes the form of a rejection of Greuze himself, as

> sentimental art is not bad only because of its ethical defects. It lacks intrinsic features that reward sustained attention and reflection. No long-term delight or satisfaction is forthcoming.[11]

Not everyone, however, shares Eaton's conviction. To be fair, Robert C. Solomon has argued that the sentimental mode constitutes moral education and a kind of rehearsal or dress rehearsal for emotional states in a less radical form than what we would encounter in reality. Sentimentality thus serves a constructive purpose.[12] Nonetheless, in the subsequent analyses, I will take Eaton's conviction to heart and begin from the assumption that the conveyed expressions and emotions are somehow out of sync with the subject matter of the paintings in question, hence causing a discrepancy between the messages of these paintings on the one hand and the expectations of the audience on the other.

Lastly, it is worth keeping in mind that any discussion of sentimentality, as per the above exchanges of opinions, involves an element of judgment. As the literary critic I. A. Richards already noted, here in a literary context:

> We cannot, obviously, judge that any response is sentimental in this sense unless we take careful account of the situation.[13]

Greuze and the Advent of Sentimentality in Painting

We can almost pinpoint the advent of sentimentality in painting, as it was the French painter Jean-Baptiste Greuze who, with his genre pieces in the second half of the eighteenth century, both renewed this genre and popularized the sentimental attitude, which also found its way into, for example, family scenes and battle scenes. Already in *Le Père de famille expliquant la Bible à ses enfants (A Father Reading the Bible to his Children)* (1755, fig. 1), exhibited at the Salon that same year, Greuze introduces an intense compositional logic, which art

10 Eaton, "Laughing at the Death of Little Nell", 277, 278.

11 Eaton, "Laughing at the Death of Little Nell", 279.

12 Robert C. Solomon, "In Defense of Sentimentality", in *Emotion and the Arts*, ed. Mette Hjort and Sue Laver (New York: Oxford University Press, 1997).

13 I. A. Richards, *Practical Criticism: A Study of Literary Judgment* (London: Kegan Paul, Trench, Trubner & Co., 1930), 258.

historian Michael Fried describes as 'a psychological and emotional extremism almost without precedent in French painting'.[14]

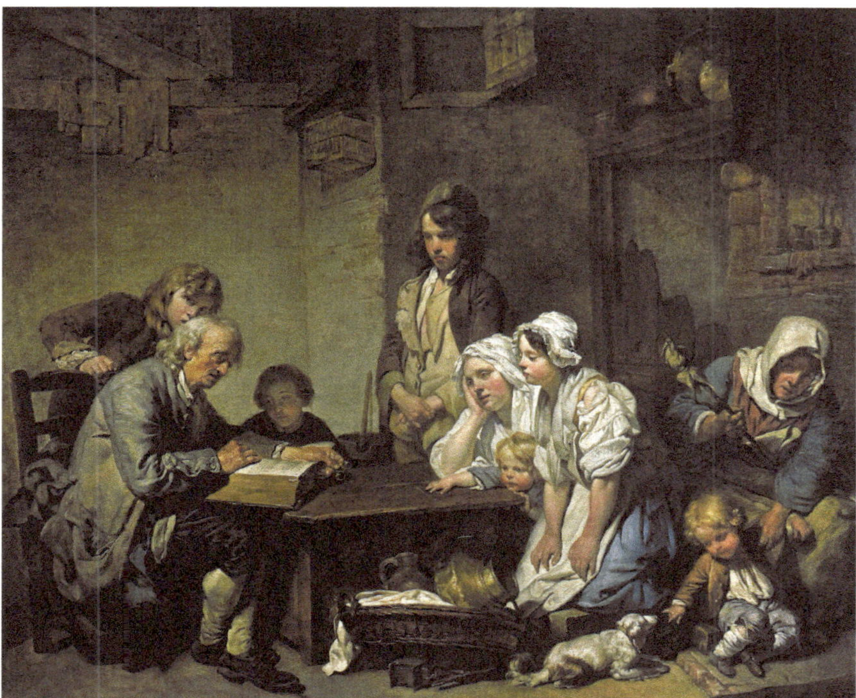

Figure 1. Jean-Baptiste Greuze, *Le Père de famille expliquant la Bible a ses enfants (A Father Reading the Bible to his Children)*, 1755. Oil on canvas, 65.3 cm × 82.4 cm (RF 2016 3), Musée du Louvre, Paris. Image courtesy of Peter Horree / Alamy Stock Photo.

In his treatise on French eighteenth-century painting, Fried attributes to Greuze (and to Jean-Baptiste-Siméon Chardin, his precursor) a renewal of narrative painting towards absorption, which he calls one pole of his famous conceptual pair. This stands in contrast to theatricality. By the former, he means works that do not have any kind of spectator appeal, where the depicted individuals are completely absorbed in inward activities or in the contemplation or communication with other figures within the pictorial space. Conversely, the theatrical denotes any attempt to have the imaginary figures address an imagined spectator. Through readings of contemporary art criticism, Fried suggests that French painting in the late eighteenth century moved away from the outward-facing

14 Michael Fried, *Absorption and Theatricality: Painting and Beholder in the Age of Diderot* (Chicago: University of Chicago Press, 1980), 10. https://doi.org/10.1525/9780520322462.

artistic ideal of the Baroque and towards a new mode, that of inwardness. Chardin had paved the way, but Greuze elevated the effect to a monumental level.[15] His works exude both staging and sentimentality, which are alien to, for example, the Flemish and Dutch tradition of genre painting that Greuze must otherwise have learned from.

With his oval paintings of young girls in sorrow and the throes of other emotions, Greuze intensified a mood of passivity, first evident in *La Simplicité (Simplicity)* (1759, Kimbell Art Museum), a work on the threshold between Rococo and Neoclassicism, and maturing in *Une Jeune fille qui a cassé son miroir (The Broken Mirror)* (c. 1762–63, Wallace Collection), and in *Une Jeune fille qui pleure son oiseau mort (Young Girl Weeping over Her Dead Bird)* (1765, Scottish National Gallery, fig. 2). The latter work was celebrated at the Salon by Diderot, who saw in the dead bird (and the shattered mirror in the preceding work) an allegory of sexual debut and lost innocence.[16] Greuze's next variation on this theme was *La Cruche cassée (The Broken Pitcher)* (1771, Louvre), thus creating a new type of genre painting.

While the bird (and birdcage) is a recurring prop in seventeenth-century Dutch genre painting, often in the hands or surroundings of young girls, with amorous or erotic significance,[17] the emotional states undergone by Greuze's girls, always in solitude, are unknown even in Dutch works with themes of unhappy love. With Diderot's characterization:

> Poor little one, how intense, how thoughtful is your pain! Why this dreamy, melancholy air? What, for a bird? You don't cry, you suffer, and your thoughts are consistent with your pain.[18]

Simultaneously, the combination of the solitary figure and the often-oval format causes the image type to oscillate between the conventions of genre painting and portrait painting. When later, in a Danish context, I incorporate the genre of portraiture, it is, among other things, with this kinship in mind.

While the absorptive impulse characterizes both Chardin and Greuze, sentimentality is a breakthrough reserved for the latter. In line with his thesis, Fried

15 'But La Porte's commentary makes clear that what he himself found most compelling about the *Père de famille* was what he saw as its persuasive representation of a particular state or condition, which each figure in the painting appeared to exemplify in his or her own way, i. e., the state or condition of rapt attention, of being completely occupied or engrossed or (as I prefer to say) absorbed in what he or she is doing, hearing, thinking, feeling.' Fried, *Absorption and Theatricality*, 10.

16 Denis Diderot, "The Salon of 1765" [1765], in *Diderot on Art*, ed. and trans. John Goodman (New Haven: Yale University Press, 1995), 1:99.

17 Wayne Franits, *Dutch Seventeenth-Century Genre Painting: Its Stylistic and Thematic Evolution* (New Haven: Yale University Press, 2004), 180.

18 Diderot, "Salon of 1765", 98.

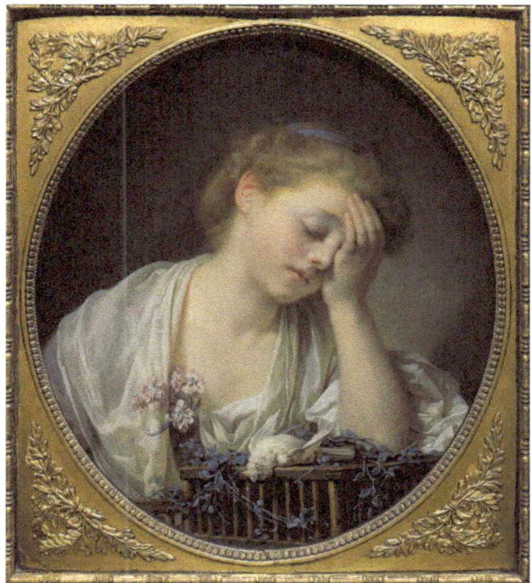

Figure 2. Jean-Baptiste Greuze, *Une Jeune fille qui pleure son oiseau mort (Young Girl Weeping over Her Dead Bird)*, 1765. Oil on canvas, 53.3 cm × 46 cm (NG 435), National Galleries of Scotland, Edinburgh. Image courtesy of photosublime / Alamy Stock Photo.

emphasizes the girl's abandonment in her sorrow as an expression of extreme self-forgetfulness. Neither the emotional intensity nor the erotic allusion can be found in Chardin's quiet world of objects and moods. Fried's juxtaposition of the two French painters culminates in an important conclusion, which also involves the status of everyday life:

> And the means by which this was accomplished suggest that by the first half of the 1760s absorption was increasingly becoming assimilated to expression rather than the other way round, as had been the case in the early and mid-1750s. Furthermore, absorption in Chardin strikes us not only as an ordinary, everyday condition but as that condition which, more than any other, characterizes ordinary, everyday experience: as the hallmark or *sine qua non* of the everyday as such. In contrast, the seeming incapacity of Greuze's figures to become absorbed in the everyday – the impression they convey of not being at home in it – accounts for our conviction that Chardin and Greuze represent different worlds.[19]

In other words, what Fried calls attention to here, in addition to the dichotomy of absorption and theatricality, is the fact that an extreme form of absorption – very much a springboard for sentimentality – emerges in the picture at the expense of the thematic embeddedness of the 'Greuze girl' into her surroundings. Figure and space seem to drift apart.

19 Fried, *Absorption and Theatricality*, 61.

As Fried does not fail to mention, the critics were just as influenced by the sentimentality of the time as the artists.[20] Diderot immersed himself so much in what he imagined must have happened before the melancholic outcome of the story that he 'recounted' the girl's imaginary love woes.

Janie Vanpée argues for framing Greuze as a modern and innovative painter (in which Fried would not disagree), not seeing sentimentality as a stumbling block but as an integrated part of this project, which, as previously noted, according to Fried, departs from everyday life and becomes pure expressive technique and virtuosity. She challenges the perception that only the subject matter, not the composition, constitutes Greuze's claim to fame and instead focuses on Greuze's thematization of gaze directions. Vanpée asserts that 'the paintings control the viewer's responses by means other than their content and meaning, and these means are still operative.' Or: 'the way our viewing is programmed within the painting itself'.[21] I will return to this 'programmed' aspect of sentimental art later, shifting the context slightly from the context of visuality to the context of emotionality.

Interestingly, Vanpée does not disagree with James Elkins' observation, made much later, that Greuze's strategy no longer holds sway over our emotions. In line with Norman Bryson's semiotic interpretation of Greuze's painterly project, she finds that the signifier and the signified have come apart, leaving only an empty – but ideologically revealing – sign in its place:

> This fissure in the painterly image voids the image of its emotional power. We continue to recognize the gestures, the movements and the glances of the figures in Greuze's paintings to be charged with emotion and drama, but they do not move us. We are attentive to these passions only as signs. As such, they appear artificial and contrived, the very opposite of the authenticity they claim. Yet, despite our alienation from these images of interpersonal drama, the paintings remain disturbing and oddly compelling, as recent, renewed interest in Greuze confirms.[22]

To some extent, the magnetic appeal of Greuze's paintings has shifted from an emotional to an intellectual level.[23] In contrast to Eaton's use of Greuze as the archetype of sentimental missteps within visual language, Vanpée attributes much greater qualities to Greuze, which are available to the viewer. Note especially her incorporation of the imagination:

20 Fried, *Absorption and Theatricality*, 59.

21 Janie Vanpée, "Jean-Baptiste Greuze: The Drama of Looking", *L'Esprit Créateur* 28, no. 4 (Winter 1988): 50.

22 Vanpée, "Jean-Baptiste Greuze", 49.

23 This conclusion also resonates with Elkins' later viewpoint, see: James Elkins, *Pictures & Tears: A History of People Who Have Cried in Front of Paintings* (New York: Routledge, 2001), 96–99. https://doi.org/10.4324/9780203990322.

> By thus framing and fueling the viewer's imagination, the 'Greuze girl' paintings introduce a temporal dimension to an essentially static art and look forward to the development of the image's potential for fantasy that the cinematic medium will exploit to the fullest. This last and clearly most controversial aspect of Greuze's art reverses the traditionally static and passive relationship of representation to its model to open it up to the active engagement of the spectator's imagination and fantasy.[24]

I will return to this dispute about Greuze, but for now, it is particularly noteworthy that Vanpée does *not* dispute that Greuze's paintings are a kind of programmatic art that, as she states, controls and programmes the beholder's approach to the works. Greuze succeeds in turning the viewer into a voyeur, as she concludes.[25]

Depictions of Children in the Early Golden Age

Many of the depictions in the early Golden Age are of children, which was a new development,[26] and it would hardly be wrong to assume that the portrayal of childhood has been a particular stumbling block for the critics of sentimentality, as exemplified by Greuze's archetypal project. Therefore, I will continue along the same lines and pursue the development in the Golden Age painters' depictions of children – mostly in genre painting, and with some excursions into portrait painting. Instead of setting forth a series of criteria for sentimentality in advance, I will let a definition gradually emerge during my analyses and comparisons, with a constant look back at the legacies of Greuze and of Fried's dichotomy.

On the threshold of the Golden Age, we find Jens Juel (1745–1802) and his free depictions of children in the spirit of the Enlightenment. Not only are children seen in more liberated, relaxed, and natural poses in Juel's portraits, which is typical of the changing perception of childhood during this period, but they are also integrated into landscape scenes in ways that are full of life and movement.[27] One of the painter's last works, *A Running Boy. Marcus Holst von Schmidten*

24 Vanpée, "Jean-Baptiste Greuze", 66.

25 Vanpée, "Jean-Baptiste Greuze", 57, 63.

26 Anna Schram Vejlby, "The themes of the exhibition: Parents and children", in *Fra den bedste side: Portræt og følsomhed i guldalderen: Keeping up Appearances: Portraits and Emotions in the Golden Age*, ed. Gertrud Oelsner and Anna Schram Vejlby (Copenhagen: The Hirschsprung Collection, 2017), 102–104.

27 'As subjects in their own right, individual children became common, so much so that they became one of the chief topics of painting. Attired in loose-fitting clothes, children were set in outdoor, natural environments, and artists strove to effect what was most charming in their small subjects. The contrast with the lack of affection shown in family portraits a century earlier could not be more marked.' Paul Duncum, *Images of Childhood: A Visual History from Stone to Screen* (London: Bloomsbury, 2023), 27. https://doi.org/10.5040/9781350299962.

(1802, National Gallery of Denmark, fig. 3), depicts the boy in a run within a landscape where the boy's school, the groundbreaking Christiani Institut with the country's first playground, can be glimpsed in the background. Both the boy's pointing gesture toward the institution he attended and his running figure make the work more than just a portrait; it is closer to an allegorical tribute to harmony between the individual, nature, and society in the spirit of enlightenment.

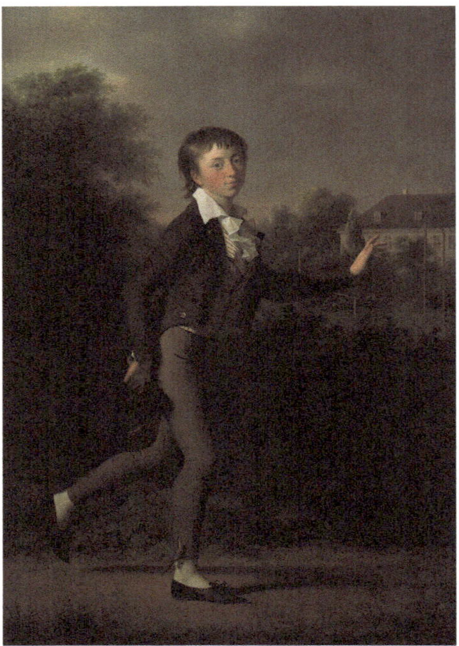

Figure 3. Jens Juel, *A Running Boy. Marcus Holst von Schmidten*, 1802. Oil on canvas, 180.5 cm x 126 cm (KMS3635), The National Gallery of Denmark, Copenhagen. Image courtesy of the National Gallery of Denmark.

The leading portrait painter of the Golden Age, Christian Albrecht Jensen (1792–1870), did not lag behind Juel in this respect. In the work *Hans and Bolette Puggaard's Three Children* (1827, The Nivaagaard Collection, fig. 4), the front boy plays the drum so that it is almost audible to the viewer, while his brother in the background has placed one hand protectively placed on his sister's shoulder, thus empathetically binding the group of figures together. This depiction of intimate bonding in pictures of siblings seems to begin in earnest with Thomas Gainsborough's (1727–1788) *The Painter's Daughters with a Cat* (c. 1760–61, National Gallery, London, fig. 5). Here, the older daughter embraces the younger one in a protective embrace. Despite Jensen's classic pyramidal grouping of the trio, the staged draperies, and a thoroughly frontal representation, not only the individualization but also the liveliness and friendliness in the children's faces make the viewer immerse herself or himself in a childlike world.

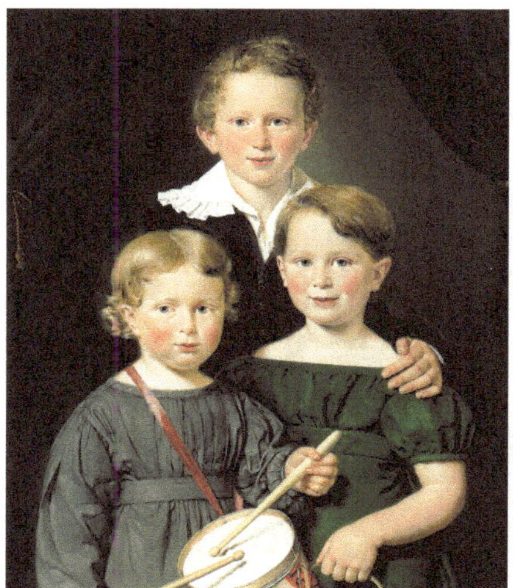

Figure 4. Christian Albrecht Jensen, *Hans and Bolette Puggaard's Three Children*, 1827. Oil on canvas, 82 cm × 64 cm (0239NMK). The Nivaagaard Collection, Nivå. Image courtesy of the Nivaagaard Collection.

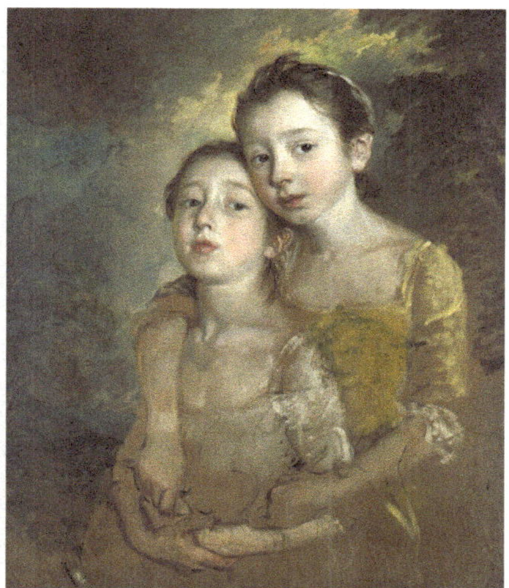

Figure 5. Thomas Gainsborough, *The Painter's Daughters with a Cat*, c. 1760–61. Oil on canvas, 75.6 cm × 62.9 cm (NG3812), National Gallery, London. Image courtesy of Archivart / Alamy Stock Photo.

A minor revolution among the budding painters at the Royal Danish Academy of Fine Arts in the second half of the 1820s led to a blossoming of genre painting. Thus, Denmark got, for the first time, a school in its own right within this genre, which had hitherto only been represented by sporadic attempts by Peter Cramer (1726–1782) and Jens Juel in the 1700s. Surprisingly, the young painters also hit the taste of the time, as many of their ambitious compositions were bought for the Royal Painting Collection. This development, where a new set of motifs, especially from the streets and salons of the capital, emerged, aligns with Kasper Monrad's determination of the period's project as driven by an interest in everyday life.[28]

A good example of a child portrait in the wake of this development is Constantin Hansen's *Three Young Girls. Study after Nature* (1827, National Gallery of Denmark, fig. 6), which, in anonymized form, depicts the painter's sisters. The work gained justified attention from the emerging art critic Niels Laurits Høyen (1798–1870) at the Charlottenborg exhibition and was immediately purchased by

28 Kasper Monrad, *Hverdagsbilleder: Dansk guldalder – kunstnerne og deres vilkår* (Copenhagen: Christian Ejlers' Forlag, 1989), 122–123.

the royal family.[29] The oval plaster relief in the window reveal to the left is cut off, and the full figures of the girls cannot fit within the frame, which arbitrarily crops them. The figures' anchoring in the crowded space becomes therefore indistinct – the floor is not seen – while the girls' absorption in needlework, drawing, and daydreaming is intensified by the painting's close-up nature. It is a work that is fully absorptive, as no gaze greets the beholder.

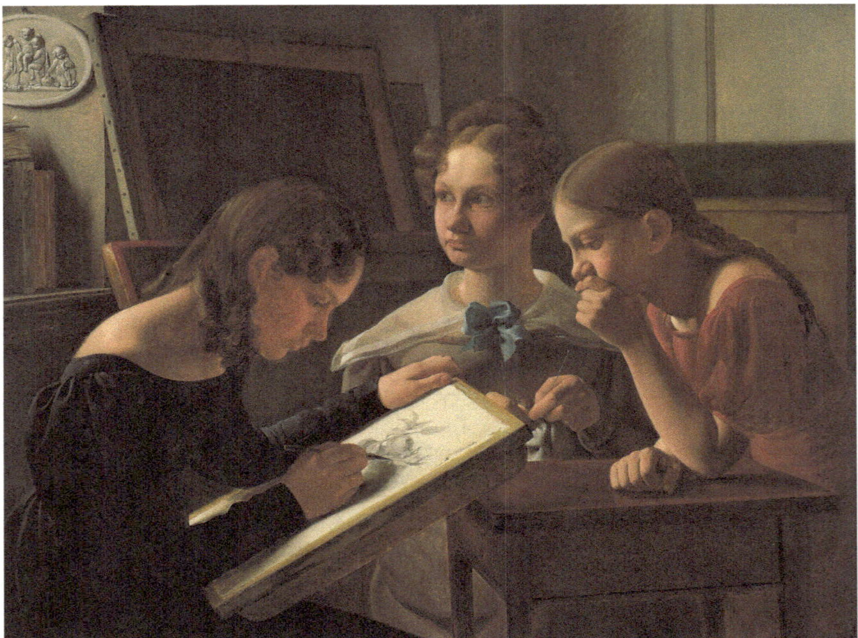

Figure 6 Constantin Hansen, *Three Young Girls. Study after Nature*, 1827. Oil on canvas, 62.5 cm × 81 cm (KMS125), The National Gallery of Denmark, Copenhagen. Image courtesy of the National Gallery of Denmark.

Also outdoors, Hansen found improvised motifs, as seen in *Street Boys Playing with Dice at Christiansborg Castle* (1834, Musée du Louvre, fig. 7). Similar to Martinus Rørbye's (1803–1848) famous street scene from *The Prison of Copenhagen* (1831, National Gallery of Denmark), Hansen plays on the contrast between the brightly dressed street boys and the bright, clearly defined palatial architecture with a solid block character. Nevertheless, the rationale of the image is to convey both the boys' age group and their widely different, individualized

29 Niels Laurits Høyen, "Nogle Bemærkninger over de paa Charlottenborg udstillede Konstsager" [1828], in *Niels Laurits Høyens Skrifter*, ed. J. L. Ussing (Copenhagen: Gyldendal, 1871), 1:69–70. https://archive.org/details/nielslauritshy01hy.

reactions to the game, namely, placed in different states of attention, presence, and absence.

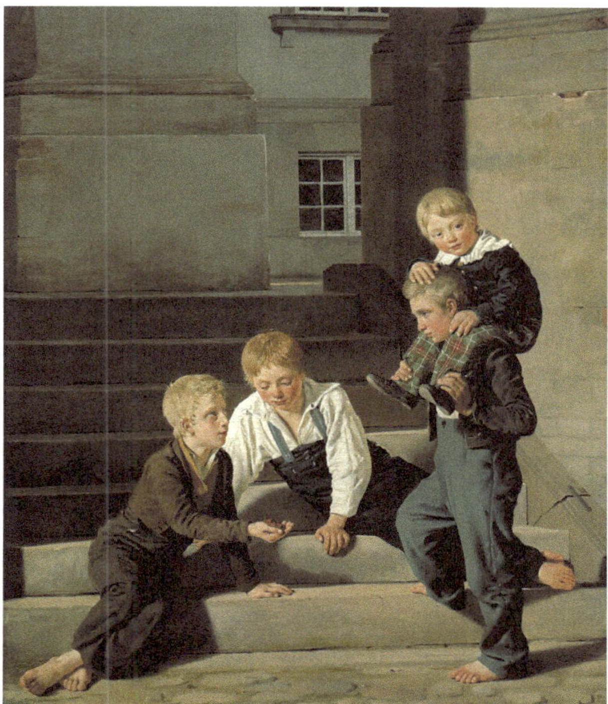

Figure 7. Constantin Hansen, *Street Boys Playing with Dice at Christiansborg Castle*, 1834. Oil on canvas, 61 cm × 50.5 cm (RF 1994 6), Musée du Louvre, Paris. Image courtesy of Painters / Alamy Stock Photo.

The same kind of emotional realism in encounters with children can be found in Wilhelm Marstrand's (1810–1873) group portrait of *The Waagepetersen Family* (1836, National Gallery of Denmark, fig. 8). Here, in a Copenhagen Biedermeier living room, we find a universe populated solely by women and children where each figure is depicted in vastly different relational positions both among themselves and towards the viewer. With the mother's white figure in the centre as the focal point, two groups of figures are seen on each side of her. To the left (the mother's right), four children are grouped around a table, engaged in playing with dolls, games, and drawing. A girl looks intensely at her doll, a boy has temporarily been distracted from his toy and looks up but still holds a ball in his hand, whereas another boy in the foreground kneels on a chair, leaning over the table, making direct eye contact with the viewer. He holds up a drawing of a man sticking out his tongue, and the boy himself has a teasing expression, providing information about his mischievous antics. Two other children, the girl on the couch and the youngest, a two- or three-year-old boy on the wet-nurse's arm, exhibit a completely different attitude – a cautious desire to participate in the fun. Finally, the largest child, a teenage girl, stands to the right in the picture and forms, together with the wet-nurse, a standing duo in contrast to all the sitting people. Both the teenage girl and her mother seem to be looking at the wet-nurse with a certain deference, although the mother might also be monitoring her baby. Marstrand has subtly indicated the teenage girl's impending journey into adulthood and her forthcoming responsibilities, and, in general, 'home is seen here from a specifically female perspective as the place of the children's rearing'.[30]

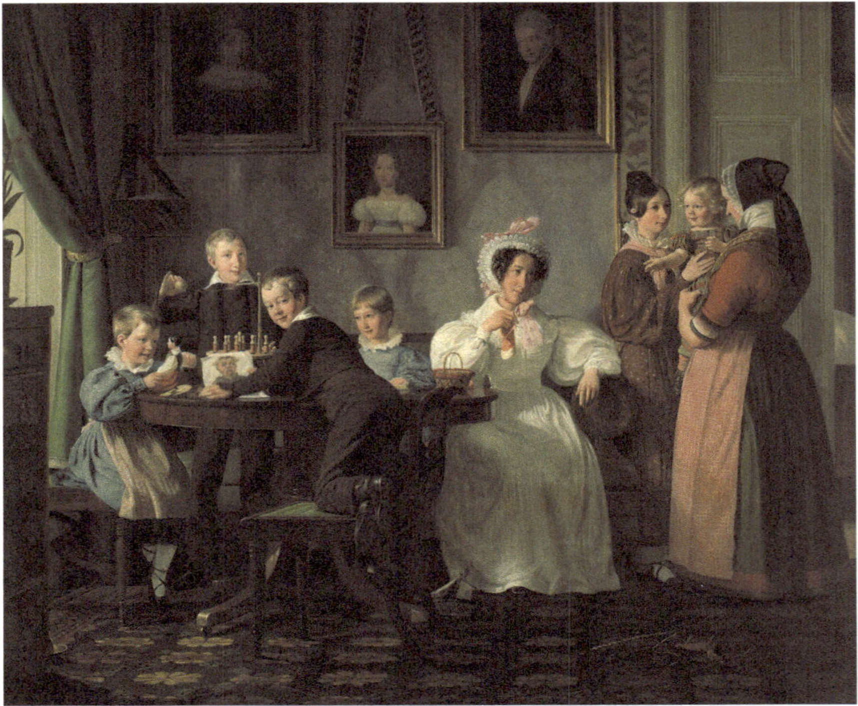

Figure 8. Wilhelm Marstrand, *The Waagepetersen Family*, 1836. Oil on canvas, 58.8 cm × 68 cm (KMS3329), The National Gallery of Denmark, Copenhagen. Image courtesy of the National Gallery of Denmark.

An excursion to Dutch Golden Age genre painting is appropriate here to put Marstrand's portrayal of children into historical perspective. If we take another work from the Dutch school and by one of its masters, Caspar Netscher (1639–

30 David Jackson, *Danish Golden Age Painting* (New Haven: Yale University Press, 2021), 113.

1684), there unfolds a similar visual complexity in *Interior with a Mother Combing her Child's Hair, Known as 'Maternal Care'* (1669, Rijksmuseum, fig. 9). The mother is occupied with the activity described in the title. Therefore, she does not notice that her daughter to the left of her sticks out her tongue at a mirror while, with one hand, pointing at her reflection (which we, of course, cannot see). However, the girl's actions have been caught by a maid in the background of the picture, who sends a disapproving look towards the girl.

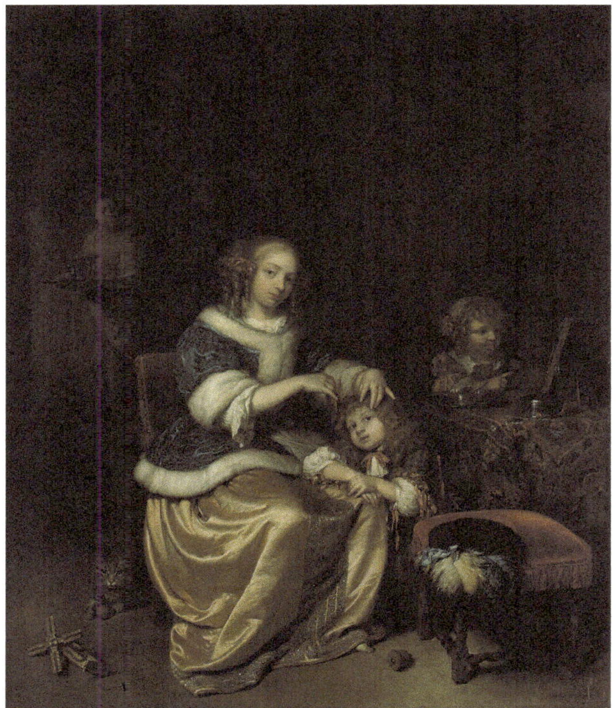

Figure 9. Caspar Netscher, *Interior with a Mother Combing her Child's Hair, Known as 'Maternal Care'*, 1669. Oil on panel, 44.5 cm × 38 cm (SK-A-293), Rijksmuseum, Amsterdam. Image courtesy of Wikimedia Commons.

The painting has been interpreted as an idealization of the harmonious household, where the daughter's play with the mirror – a prop associated with vanity – is behaviour that might soon be corrected by the maid's intervention so that harmony – i. e., on the terms of the adults – can be restored. Conversely, the toys on the floor and the ongoing play of the cat attest that childhood has a great space for expression here.[31]

31 Mariët Westermann, "'Costly and Curious, Full off Pleasure and home contentment': *Making*

In Netscher's ambiguous family scene, the daughter's gestures not only confirm to the viewer that she is sitting in front of a mirror but also that we are faced with an amusing situation. However, were it not for the disciplining gaze of the maid, both the girl's compositional isolation and her engagement in play would have encapsulated her world as an independent domain, isolated from the control of the adult world. For this is the nature of child's play.[32]

This play with the role of the viewer and the relational dynamics in the image is characteristic of the most ambitious Dutch genre painting as it developed after c. 1650. Figures that seem to 'comment on' the action are also present.[33] Through these spatial or gestural techniques, one can, in the most advanced of these works, get a sense of events that have preceded the depicted scene or events that are in the making. Often, the condition for the painters' extension of the narrative is the spatial arrangement of the images, possibly with another cast of characters. Art historian Martha Hollander has convincingly argued that the spatial doubling allows this to happen:

> The 'secondary scene' can serve rhetorically as an ancillary image, a way to enrich the scene with antithesis, parallel, irony, or explanation.[34]

Most Danish Golden Age works do not possess such complexity. Nevertheless, Marstrand's individualization of appearance, activity level, and personality, even in children, testifies to more than a schematic or stereotypical approach to the child's world as an artistic challenge. Motifs of movement play a crucial role in characterizing each child as an individual, just as they do in, for example, Jan Steen's (1625/26–1679) *Children Frying Pancakes* (c. 1665, Nivaagaard Collection, fig. 10).

This sense of extended spatiality or temporality outlined by Hollander plays a role both in the assessment of the credibility of a figurative, naturalistic image and in the degree of capacity the image possesses to activate our imagination. Philosopher Kendall L. Walton, in his seminal work on the presuppositions and mechanisms of visual art, has emphasized that all representational art, whether it is a realistic novel or a figurative painting, operates by virtue of an affinity with our

Home in the Dutch Republic", in *Art & Home: Dutch Interiors in the Age of Rembrandt*, ed. Marlene Chambers and Mariët Westermann (Zwolle: Waanders Publishers, 2001), 47, 67.

32 'In general, however much games are in essence representations and however much the players represent themselves in them, games are not presented for anyone – i. e., they are not aimed at an audience. Children play for themselves, even when they represent.' Hans-Georg Gadamer, *Truth and Method*, trans. Joel Weinsheimer and Donald G. Marshall (London: Continuum, 2006), 108.

33 Jochen Becker, "Beholding the Beholder: the Reception of 'Dutch' Painting", *Argumentation* 7 (1993): 73. https://doi.org/10.1007/BF00735043.

34 Martha Hollander, *An Entrance for the Eyes: Space and Meaning in Seventeenth-Century Dutch Art* (Berkeley, CA: University of California Press, 2002), 46.

world of imagination. We pretend that we are confronted with a real scenario – or rather, one that could well be real: an *as-if* reality. This relationship allows for some significant deviations from reality, such as when we, by our own imaginative power, fill in the gaps in a textual narrative – for there will always be a lack of total information about all individuals' actions – and similarly fill in the narrative gaps in a visual story.[35]

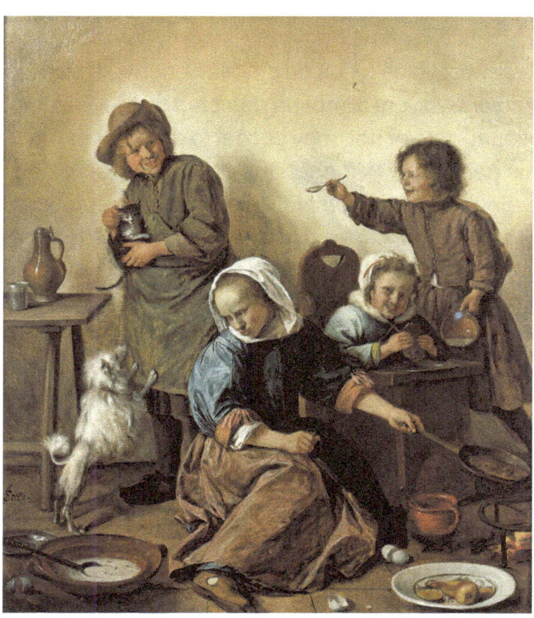

Figure 10. Jan Steen, *Children Frying Pancakes*, c. 1665. Oil on panel, 82 cm × 70.5 cm (0054NMK), The Nivaagaard Collection, Nivå. Image courtesy of the Nivaagaard Collection.

The classical objections against sentimentality in art point to the fact that the work, regardless of its medium, partly fails to stimulate curiosity because it leaves no room for the reader's or viewer's independent mental or imaginative intervention. Also, due to its banality (shared with the phenomenon of kitsch), it does not offer a lasting aesthetic experience. Although Walton's theory is aimed at figurative and realistic art in general and is not intended to explain sentimentality, the theory indirectly provides a starting point for an explanatory model for the deficiency of sentimentality as an aesthetic strategy.

Other explanatory paths can be sought in theories of the emotions. In his exploration of the transmission of emotions through art, philosopher William

35 Kendall L. Walton, *Mimesis as Make-Believe: On the Foundations of the Representational Arts* (Cambridge, MA: Harvard University Press, 1990), 45–46, 66.

Lyons has proposed seven categories to gauge who feels what – the sender (artist) or the receiver (beholder), or both parties? He also asks whether the emotions are explicitly depicted in the work (as in Edvard Munch's *The Scream* (1893), which simultaneously documents an affective state in the artist) and whether they can be generated, intentionally or not, by the work. The categories range from a starting point where the source of emotions is the artist himself or herself to a point where the emotions can no longer be detected in the work but can only be associatively linked to it.[36]

In contrast to his two first categories which focus on emotions derived from the psyche of the painter, Lyons' third one covers 'Emotion *depicted by* the Painting. The painter, whether in an emotional state or not, may set out to depict or express some emotion or emotions in his painting.'[37] Although the previous examples of genre and portrait painting have not been made solely to convey an emotional state, both *Hans and Bolette Puggaard's Three Children* and *The Waagepetersen Family* portray children in various states of joy and happiness. Their state of joy might rub off on us as spectators as well, yet it would be wrong to claim that the paintings have been created in order to transport us as beholders into a particular emotional state. By virtue of being portrait paintings, their function was never primarily emotional. Instead, the various emotional states have been used by the painters to characterize the children and their personalities.

The fact that these painters' uses of emotions serve the subject matter rather than the viewer is not the sole explanation for the perceived authenticity of these pictures, however. The works under discussion range from depicting absorptive states of isolation to depicting expressive states of mutual play and interaction. Various props and/or interiors have been called upon to contextualize or even characterize these children. Lastly, Hansen's two pictures centre on very different, yet realistically depicted, activities and atmospheres, just as he is equally adept at capturing typical childlike behaviour whether inside or outside of the home.

None of the previous Danish Golden Age paintings can claim to be free from idealization, but unlike sentimental types of images, idealization is not found in an emotional outburst but rather in composition, accessories, bright colours, possibly embellished faces of the children, etc. At the same time, it is worth noting that, with the exception of Hansen's depiction of street boys, all the works were created on commission and were not intended for an anonymous art market. There is nothing peculiar about this, as one can observe a classic difference between portrait art and genre art. This is mentioned here just to emphasize that

36 William Lyons, "On Looking into Titian's *Assumption*", in *Emotion and the Arts*, ed. Mette Hjort and Sue Laver (New York: Oxford University Press, 1997), 143.

37 Lyons, "On Looking into Titian's *Assumption*", 143.

the difference, both in terms of genre and in terms of intended target group, does not affect the painters' ability to weave realistic feelings and reactions into the interplay between the figures.

Depictions of Children in the Late Golden Age

If we seek out more images of children, now from the late Golden Age, then Peter Julius Larsen's (1818–1852) *Two Poor Children* (1845, National Gallery of Denmark, fig. 11) is a good starting point for discussion. It was purchased by the royal family directly from the Charlottenborg Exhibition the same year. Two poor children gather firewood in the forest, accompanied by a dog. The portrayal of poor children is not new, but the innovations in Larsen's work compared to previous depictions of children consist partly in the fact that the children are alone, left to themselves, as if it were a portrait, and partly in the direct, resigned gaze with which the boy meets the viewer. The accompanying dog warms itself by the girl's lap, but it is evidently too cold for her to expose her hands – which she hides under a shawl – to pet the dog.

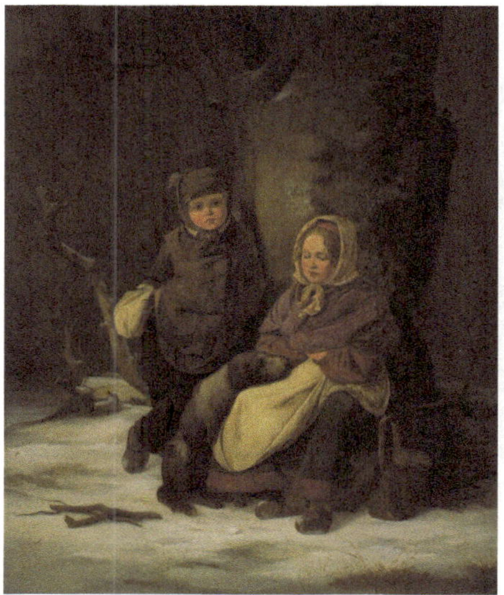

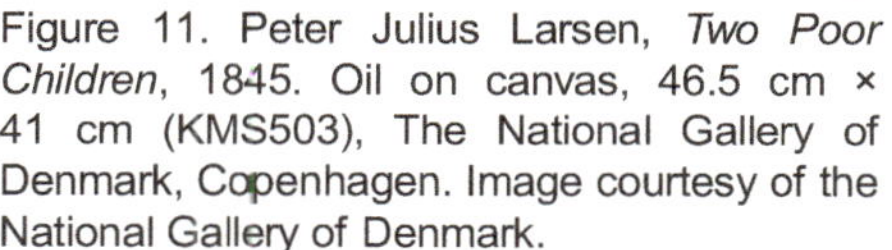

Figure 11. Peter Julius Larsen, *Two Poor Children*, 1845. Oil on canvas, 46.5 cm × 41 cm (KMS503), The National Gallery of Denmark, Copenhagen. Image courtesy of the National Gallery of Denmark.

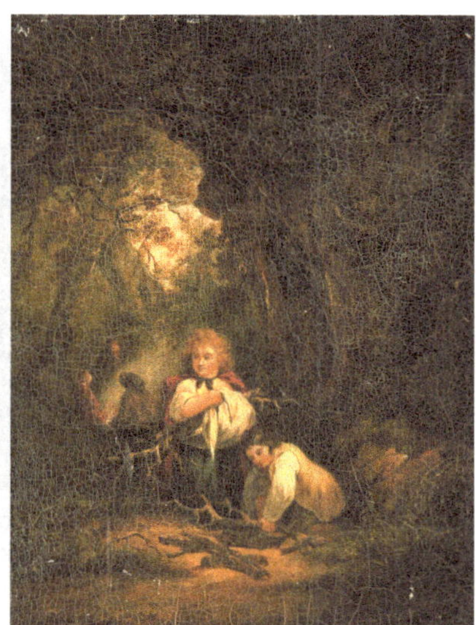

Figure 12. George Morland, *Gathering Wood*, undated. Oil on panel, 40.3 cm × 32 cm (A296), Torre Abbey Museum, Torquay. Image courtesy of Art UK.

A similar depiction is difficult to find in the seventeenth-century Dutch school, which was otherwise accessible in the form of partially public painting collections in Copenhagen and apparently served as a frame of reference for some of the Danish Golden Age painters.[38] A larger work from the period, Jan de Bray's (1627–1697) *Caring for the Children at the Orphanage in Haarlem: Three Acts of Mercy* (1663, Frans Hals Museum, fig. 13), shows children with uplifted eyes receiving clothes, food, and drink. Providence is responsible for the children's fate here. Conversely, in Larsen's painting, where the children's future seems to rely on our compassion and potential intervention.

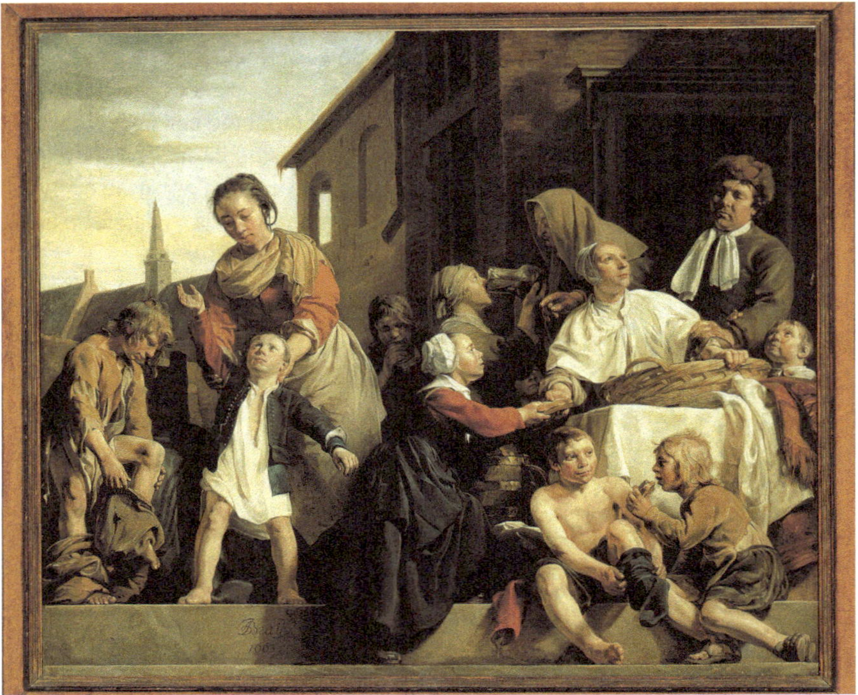

Figure 13. Jan de Bray, *Caring for the Children at the Orphanage in Haarlem: Three Acts of Mercy*, 1663. Oil on canvas, 132.5 cm 154 cm (os I-31), Frans Hals Museum, Haarlem. Photographer: René Gerritsen, Image courtesy of Frans Hals Museum.

38 Lene Bøgh Rønberg, "Bourgeois Home Life in the Two Golden Ages – influences and correspondences", in *Two Golden Ages: Masterpieces of Dutch and Danish Painting*, ed. Lene Bøgh Rønberg, Kasper Monrad, and Ragni Linnet, trans. W. Glyn Jones (Amsterdam/Copenhagen: Rijksmuseum/The National Gallery of Denmark, 2001), 100, 107–108, 116, 119, 126. Flemish and Dutch art was also highly regarded by Høyen, see: Rønberg, "Bourgeois Home Life in the Two Golden Ages", 77.

Another example can illustrate how radically different Larsen's project is compared to his predecessors from two hundred years earlier. In a series of variations on the same theme, Jacob Ochtervelt (1634–1682) depicted a clash between rich and poor. *Street Musicians at the Door* (1665, Saint Louis Art Museum, fig. 14) is symptomatic in this regard. Here, Ochtervelt has simply reserved the luminous and elegant world for the domestic interior, while the street lies in gloomy darkness. The musicians are dressed in dirty rags, but typical of the approach of the time, the painter has endowed the poor with laughter and cheerfulness – the misery itself is kept at bay, at least on canvas. The same tendency toward merriment amid apparent misery can be observed in countless tavern scenes by Jan Steen.

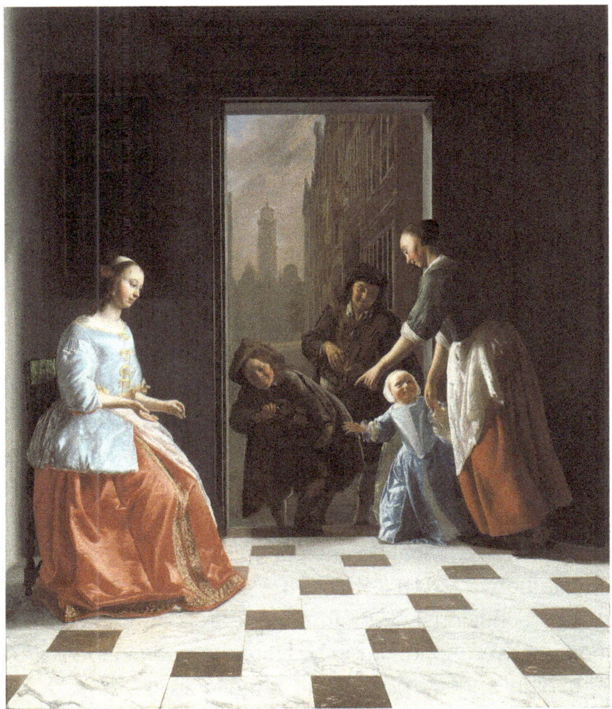

Figure 14. Jacob Ochtervelt, *Street Musicians at the Door*, 1665. Oil on canvas, 68.5 cm × 57.1 cm (162:1928), Saint Louis Art Museum, St. Louis, Missouri. Image courtesy of Wikimedia Commons.

Finally, one can compare Larsen's painting to a series of thematically similar works by the extremely popular English genre painter George Morland (1763–1804). One of Morland's recurring themes is peasants or gypsies gathering firewood in the forest in autumn or winter. But in his works, neither the desperation nor the isolation that Larsen employs can be seen. A typical example is *Gathering Wood* (undated, Torre Abbey Museum, fig. 12), where the two wood gatherers have an air of thrift and contentment, while the shadows of a group of figures can be seen around a fire in the background. The gaze toward the viewer is also alien to Morland's practice, which, in a classical manner, instead creates a network of interconnected gazes inward into the pictorial space.

Martinus Rørbye was the first artist to explore the coastal town of Skagen as a thematic workspace, and this happened as early as 1834. At that time, painters like Morland had been busy painting beach scenes with idyllic fishermen for half a century. Soon after, the beach became a preferred motif in the late Golden Age, and the depiction of children also found its way here. Christian Andreas Schleisner's (1810–1882) *Children Sheltering from the Storm* (1854, private collection, fig. 15) is symptomatic of one form of child depiction in the period. The work is sophisticated because the children, who have taken shelter in a boat, react to a danger that we cannot see: The storm is in the distance, outside the picture frame. This device is seen in several fishing scenes from the period, including those by both Rørbye and Peter Raadsig (1806–1882) who, in *Beach Scene from Old Skagen with an Impending Storm* (1834, Ny Carlsberg Glyptotek) and *Storm on the West Coast of Jutland* (1853, private collection) respectively, portray the assembled characters fearing a shipwreck we can only guess at, not see.

Nevertheless, this complexity does not compensate for the fact that we are faced with radically different depictions of children than the older models. Here, the children are isolated and made pawns for external threats of various kinds. The portrait-like depiction with static and sometimes statuary features suggests, on the one hand, an independence, which on the other hand is immediately undermined by the children's passivity and helplessness. At the same time, Schleisner's beach has a non-place quality: Despite the contemporaneous preoccupation with topographical identification and communication, as seen, for example, in Johan Thomas Lundbye (1818–1848) or Peter Christian Skovgaard (1817–1875), Schleisner has consciously kept the image free of markers that could characterize the location even approximately. Here, he goes in the opposite direction of the desire to paint specific places and inhabitants in Denmark, as formulated by Niels Laurits Høyen, and which became the norm for a considerable part of the late Golden Age genre painting.[39]

A painter who, more than any other embraced the beach scene as a preferred subject, was Julius Friedlænder (1810–1861), who was also extremely popular in

39 Niels Laurits Høyen, "Om Betingelserne for en Skandinavisk Nationalkonsts Udvikling" [1844], in *Niels Laurits Høyens Skrifter*, ed. J. L. Ussing (Copenhagen: Gyldendal, 1871), 1:351–368. https://archive.org/details/nielslauritshy01hy.

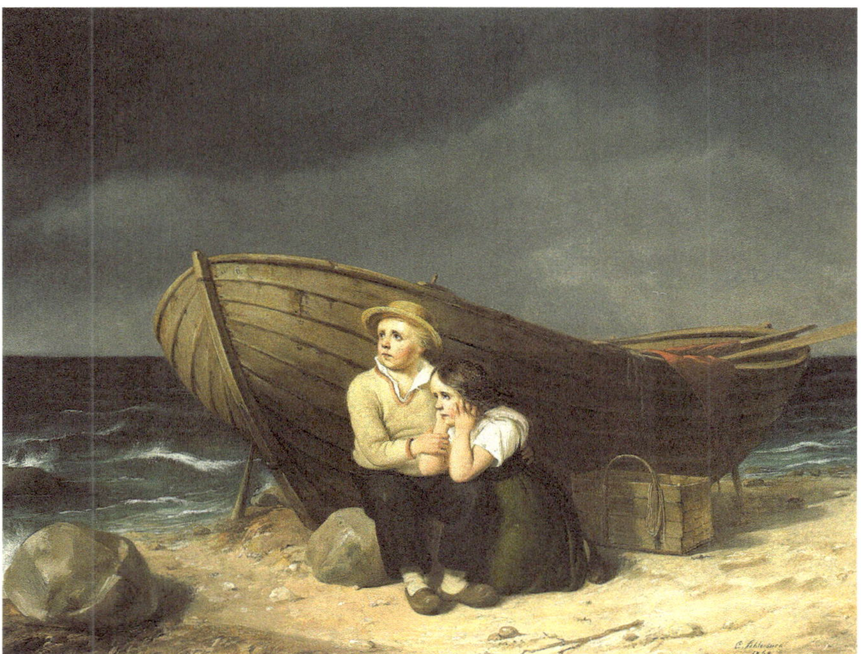

Figure 15. Christian Andreas Schleisner, *Children Sheltering from the Storm*, 1854. Oil on canvas, 41 cm × 53 cm, private collection. Image courtesy of Wikimedia Commons.

the art market. He often chose the coasts of North Zealand as his aesthetic domain. Compared to Schleisner, Friedlænder's coastal childhood scenes typically play on a larger register, including a detailed depiction of children's improvised play. *Fishermen's Children with a Cockchafer* (1854, exhibited at Charlottenborg the same year, private collection, fig. 16) is a good example, both convincing and acknowledging a child's world as a phenomenon in its own right. However, it resembles Schleisner's and Larsen's approaches in one aspect, namely the tendency toward portrait-like isolation. Behind the two children, we are presented with a gaze out to sea towards infinity, only interrupted by a tiny sailboat in the distance and a diffuse rocky coastline farthest back. Again, one can compare with Morland, who in his *Calm off the Coast of the Isle of Wight* (c. 1799–1804, Leicester Museum and Art Gallery, fig. 17) shows individuals deeply integrated into a characteristic and expansive landscape full of landmarks and activity.

One way to stage emotions in painting is to show us an emotional *reaction* to an event. Here, I think primarily of an interaction between figures. Greuze's breakthrough work, *A Father Reading the Bible to his Children*, shows figures absorbed in an emotional state in response to the reading, although the listeners

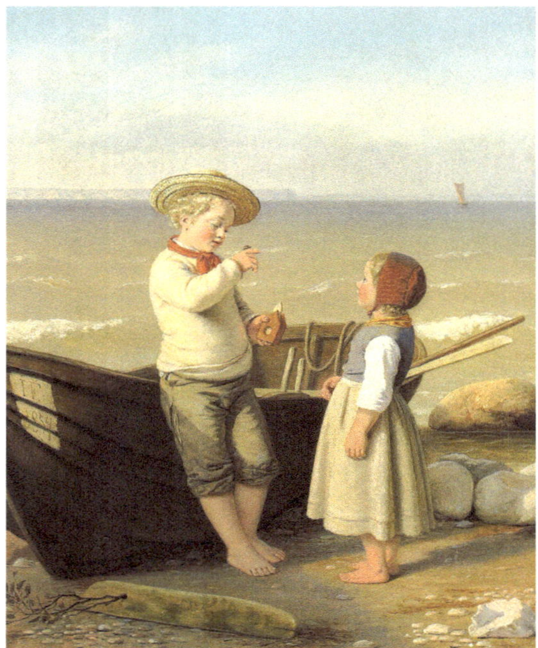

Figure 16. Julius Friedlænder, *A Fisherman's Children with a Cockchafer*, 1854. Oil on canvas, 57 cm × 48 cm, private collection. Image courtesy of Wikimedia Commons.

are passive. And Caravaggio's *Boy Bitten by a Lizard* (1594–96, Fondazione Roberto Longhi) which, with its exploration of the emotional response to pain in one individual was innovative, would fall squarely within Lyons' third category, 'Emotion *depicted by* the Painting'.[40]

However, with Larsen and Schleisner, we only encounter an appeal out of the picture plane, towards the viewer – *not* an exchange of emotions between figures in the picture. The complex facial expressions and gestures that knit the composition together into a unity in the paintings of children by Hansen and Marstrand are completely absent.

Larsen and Schleisner are not alone in this strategy, which marks the return of theatricality, to express it in Fried's terms. In an earlier, peripheral work by the relatively unknown painter (and fallen soldier) Sophus Schack (1811–1864), *Poor Children Singing in a Courtyard on a Winter's Day* (1838, Thorvaldsen's Museum, fig. 18), the same thing happens. Both the three children and the surroundings are depicted in tatters and in dismal decay, and a factory chimney

40 Lisa Beaven, "The Visual Arts", in *A Cultural History of the Emotions in the Baroque and Enlightenment Age*, ed. Claire Walker, Katie Barclay, and David Lemmings (London: Bloomsbury Academic, 2019), 87. https://doi.org/10.5040/9781474207041.ch-005.

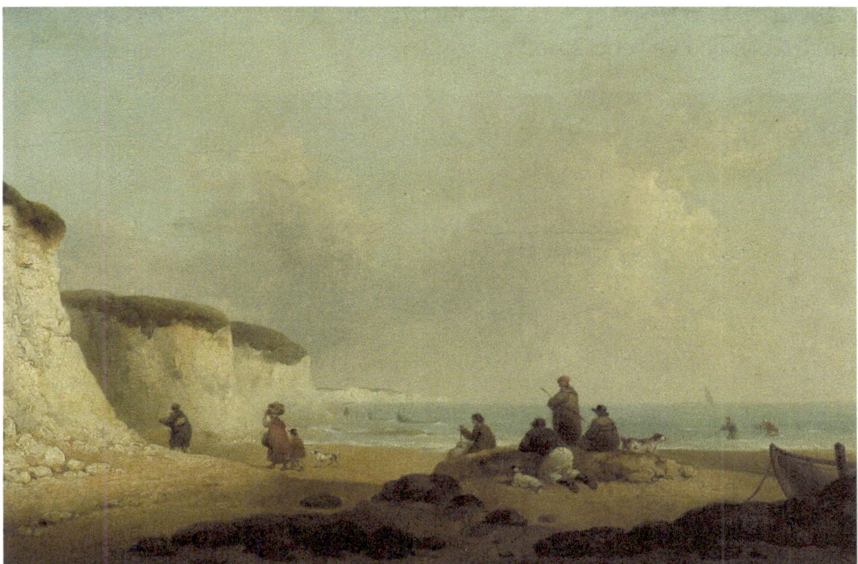

Figure 17. George Morland, *Calm off the Coast of the Isle of Wight*, c. 1799–1804. Oil on panel, 27.6 × 40.7 cm (L.F7.1890.0.0), Leicester Museum and Art Gallery, Leicester. Image courtesy of Bridgeman Images.

in the background cements the sad surroundings, in case one should happen to doubt the pervasive misery. Communicatively, the children have no internal coherence, and they appear as three soloists. Who are they singing for? Us as the audience, naturally. The use of intermediary figures in the foreground, for example, of saints or patrons, which began to characterize modern painting in the Renaissance and which later evolved into complex relationships between figures possibly shifted in time, is completely eliminated here. In Wolfgang Kemp's aesthetics of reception such secondary figures are called 'vehicles of identification' and serve as 'focalizers who can address the beholder directly'.[41]

Interestingly, one of the very few documentable contemporary attacks on sentimentality in Danish Golden Age painting, by the writer Meïr Aron Goldschmidt (1819–1887) in his review of the 1850 Charlottenborg Exhibition, concerns not only a painting by Schack, but also a painting of children (*Genii Leading*

41 Wolfgang Kemp, "The Work of Art and Its Beholder: The Methodology of the Aesthetic of Reception", in *The Subjects of Art History: Historical Objects in Contemporary Perspectives*, ed. Mark A. Cheetham, Michael Ann Holly and Keith Moxey, trans. Astrid Heyer and Michael Ann Holly (Cambridge: Cambridge University Press, 1998 [Cologne 1985]), 187.

a Dying Child to Heaven).[42] 'To such Materialism, a sentimental Spiritualism can lead', Goldschmidt concludes.[43]

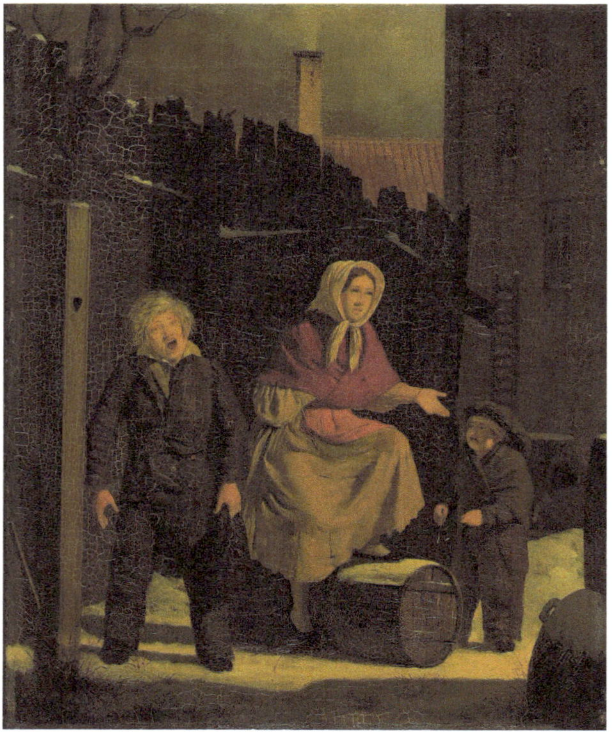

Figure 18. Sophus Schack, *Poor Children Singing in a Courtyard on a Winter's Day*, 1838. Oil on canvas, 36.5 cm × 29.2 cm (B288), Thorvaldsen Museum, Copenhagen. Image courtesy of Thorvaldsen's Museum.

Defining Sentimentality in Works of Art

If we truly are to grasp the sea change of the new mode of depicting children during the late Golden Age, we have to return to Lyons' categories. Particularly relevant to the undertaking here is his category number four:

42 Exhibited as no. 159. *Fortegnelse over de ved det Kongelige Akademie for de skiönne Kunster offentlig udstillede Kunstværker* (Copenhagen: Thiele, 1850), 12.

43 'Til en Saadan Materialisme kan en sentimental Spiritualisme føre.' Meïr Aron Goldschmidt, "Noget om Kunstudstillingen", in *Nord og Syd. Et Ugeskrift*, ed. Meïr Aron Goldschmidt 4 (April–June 1850): 190. https://archive.org/details/nordgsyd06goldgoog. It has neither been possible to locate the whereabouts of this painting nor find a reproduction of it.

> Emotion *generated through* the Painting. The painter may set out, via his painting, but not via the depiction or expression in it of some emotion, to generate a particular emotion or emotions in a viewer.[44]

Lyons' cardinal example of this strategy, which – as is clearly evident – is deliberately orchestrated by the artist, is a sentimental genre painting, Sir John Everett Millais' (1829–1896) *The Blind Girl* (1854–56, Birmingham Museum and Art Gallery, fig. 19), typical of Victorian taste. Here, a red-haired girl is depicted sitting with closed eyes by the roadside in a lush landscape with fields and a double rainbow in the background. She has a smaller, blonde girl in her lap, whom she holds by the hand – presumably her sister. The older girl has closed eyes in her pretty face, warmed by the sun. The expression could indicate a state of rest, but the title of the painting gives the viewer the sad certainty that she is blind. The same is confirmed by the tell-tale sign ('Pity the Blind') she wears around her neck. The rest of her body language also alludes to this while simultaneously constituting a kind of allegory of the senses in the Dutch manner. Her free hand is picking a flower (touch), and in her lap, she holds an accordion (hearing). Both rainbows and a colourful butterfly perched on her cape thematize a richness of colours (sight). Yet only her seeing companion can behold and appreciate these marvels. As Lyons notes, the musical instrument signals that the blind girl is relegated to a life as a busker. 'Nothing is left to the imagination', observes Lyons disapprovingly, while his remaining examples, sourced from Baroque religious painting and propaganda alike, indicate a tendency towards emotional exaggeration and a form of painted programme.[45] Historian of childhood Paul Duncum mentions children 'pictured in situations and with expressions that were carefully calculated to elicit a furtive tear'.[46]

Naturally, emotions are not absent in sentimental paintings – children are precisely distressed or powerless – but the rationale of the works is not to *illustrate* an emotion but to *evoke* it.[47] For the same reason, the spatiality or context in the pictures is often secondary or rudimentary, and typically one senses no atmosphere between space and figure, as the evocation of an atmosphere – which is always more diffuse than an emotion – could cast doubt on the identification or communication of a given feeling. As with Juel, the landscape serves an allegorical purpose in Millais but now mainly to delineate a handicap, no longer as a symbolic characterization of the protagonist, nor of society and its norms (as in Bruegel's pioneering works). Or, to be precise, we are faced with a symbolic characterization in reverse, and, in fact, the construal of a symbolic

44 Lyons, "On Looking into Titian's *Assumption*", 143.
45 Lyons, "On Looking into Titian's *Assumption*", 146–147.
46 Duncum, *Images of Childhood*, 29.
47 Lyons, "On Looking into Titian's *Assumption*", 147.

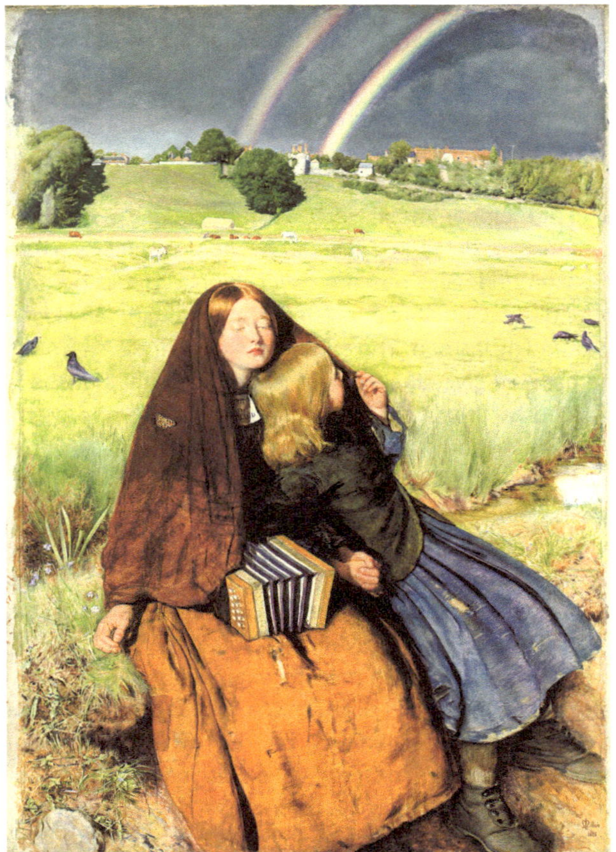

Figure 19. Sir John Everett Millais, *The Blind Girl*, 1854–56. Oil on canvas, 83 cm × 62 cm (1892P3), Birmingham Museum and Art Gallery, Birmingham. Image courtesy of Birmingham Museums Trust.

landscape in the service of a unified emotional message to the beholder confirms its novelty precisely because its intensely emotional communication deviates from past precedent. Thus, although Millais' emotive communication clearly extends beyond the direct appeal preferred by Larsen and Schack, involving a larger and more subtle register, his tendency to instrumentally subsume the entirety of the picture plane to one emotion only – that of pity – is sentimental to the bone, as is the consciousness of the beholder that this procedure entails.

By comparison, one can again think of Munch's *The Scream*, which actually falls into two of Lyons' categories because it both conveys an experienced feeling ('Emotion *transferred from* the Painter') and depicts a state of emotion

('Emotion *depicted by* the Painting'). Sentimental painting does neither, at least not as its primary task.

Lyons does not elaborate on his notion of the 'programming' of emotions in art, but Kemp's aesthetics of reception might be of assistance if we are to arrive at an operational notion of sentimentality in art. Already in his plea for a reception aesthetics modelled on certain notions from literary theory, Kemp introduces 'the *blank* or the aesthetics of *indeterminacy*' as a key term:[48]

> This state of unfinishedness or indeterminacy is constructed and intentional. But it does mean that as spectators we must complete the invisible reverse side of each represented figure, or that we mentally continue a path that is cut off by the frame. In this way, everyday perception is no different from aesthetic perception. The work of art lays a claim to coherence, though, and this impulse turns its 'blanks' into important links or causes for constituting meaning.[49]

While not laying claim to having demystified once and for all the issue of sentimentality in art, I propose that Kemp has provided us with an explanatory key of great value for unravelling exactly this question. In conjunction with the visual 'programmedness' thematized by Vanpée and the ethical lack of sincerity identified by Eaton, Kemp's notion of the blank sheds light on the functioning of the sentimental picture. In another key text, in which he puts the 'constitutive blank' into perspective by analysing paintings by Pierre-Paul Prud'hon (1758–1823) and Jean-Léon Gérôme (1824–1904), Kemp asserts the following:

> These relationships can be so constituted that blanks postpone of impede connection of a picture's constitutive elements, making perception of the picture difficult or disrupting it, even making the blanks themselves independent and displaying their wilfulness at the expense of the ideal of problem-free communication.[50]

I will not go into details here, as it would take me too far from the present subject matter, but merely state that Kemp here indexes both various types of blanks and several ways of using blanks in a composition in more or less radical ways. As the nineteenth century drew to a close, the modern painter would forsake the 'law of intelligibility', as Kemp calls it – 'instead he arranges spaces and surfaces, which are open to the projective activity of the beholder'.[51] In more than one way, the stereotypical sentimental picture of the nineteenth century seems to go against this trend, leaving no blanks for the beholder to ponder. For the emotional impact takes precedence in this type of picture, often relegating pictorial devices to the background, whereas in modern painting they were beginning to become the

48 Kemp, "The Work of Art and Its Beholder", 188.
49 Kemp, "The Work of Art and Its Beholder", 188.
50 Wolfgang Kemp and Raymond Meyer, trans., "Death at Work: A Case Study on Constitutive Blanks in Nineteenth-Century Painting", *Representations* 10 (Spring, 1985): 109.
51 Kemp and Meyer, "Death at Work", 102, 114.

very centres of attraction. This is not to endorse a Greenbergian formalist view of painting but merely to state the obvious.[52] In other words, if the experimental, proto-avant-garde paintings of the nineteenth century increasingly exposed the conditions of their making as well as called into question the traditional role of the spectator, the typical sentimental picture of the same period did the opposite, programming the canvas to better trigger the desired reaction, albeit based on a new culture of emotions that allowed for an instrumentalization hitherto unseen.

The sentimental paintings of children by Larsen, Schleisner, and Schack testify to a shift in both compositional logic and mood, which particularly manifest in a direct or indirect relation of address to the viewer. Either we are met by the pleading eyes' appeal for compassion or the protagonists are depicted in a situation of helplessness or powerlessness without any help seeming near (in the form of other potential figures). In both cases, the absorption, which Fried has made the litmus test for a modern attitude, is completely absent, which is why the paintings do not actually resemble Greuze's. Here, the girls are transported into a state of reverie, of self-forgetfulness or self-absorption.[53] But in the isolating mode and in the preference for placelessness, they resemble Greuze's prototype for the sentimental picture.

For the sake of comparison, Bartolomé Esteban Murillo's (1617–1682) *Children Eating Grapes and a Melon* (c. 1645, Alte Pinakothek, fig. 20) features only internal glances and gazes. We find here neither an appeal to the beholder nor a narrative that ventures beyond the picture frame. When Hegel praised this work in his *Lectures on Aesthetics*, it was precisely due to the presence of qualities that would – following Fried – later evolve into the pure state of absorption:

> But in this poverty and semi-nakedness what precisely shines forth within and without is nothing but complete absence of care and concern – a Dervish could not have less – in the full feeling of their well-being and delight in life. This freedom from care for external things and the inner freedom made visible outwardly is what the Concept of the Ideal requires.[54]

Here it is worth noting, as Anne Higonnet has done in her study of childhood innocence, that while the standard Baroque depiction of children bore the imprint of belonging to a clearly defined class (as evidenced by Murillo's work and contemporary portraits of nobility), the Romantic renditions show us children that 'have no class'.[55] In such works, derived from Sir Joshua Reynolds' (1723–1792)

52 Jonathan Crary, "Nineteenth-Century Visual Incapacities", in *Visual Literacy*, ed. James Elkins (New York: Routledge, 2009), 60. https://doi.org/10.4324/9780203957460.

53 Fried, *Absorption and Theatricality*, 13.

54 G. W. F. Hegel, *Aesthetics: Lectures on Fine Art*, trans. T. M. Knox (Oxford: Clarendon Press, 1975), 1:170.

55 Anne Higonnet, *Pictures of Innocence: The History and Crisis of Ideal Childhood* (London: Thames & Hudson, 1998), 24.

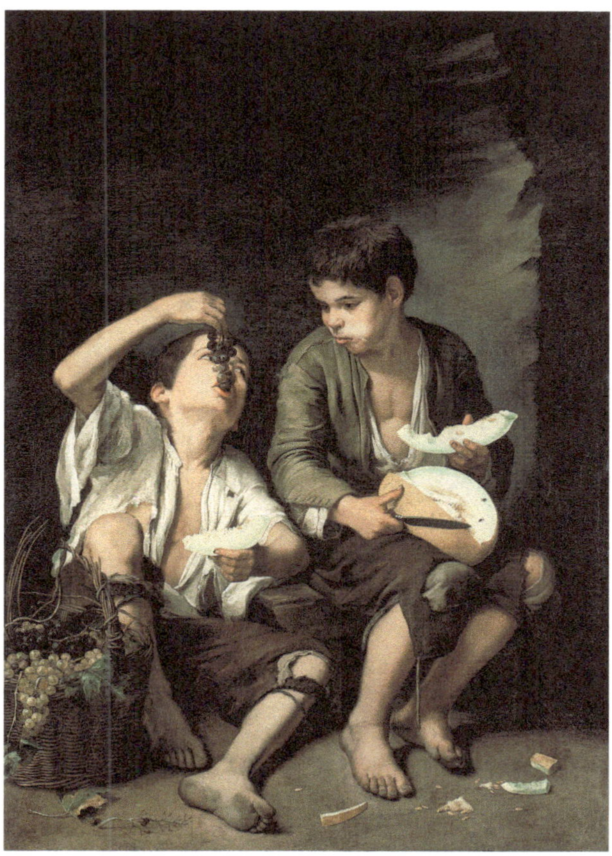

Figure 20. Bartolomé Esteban Murillo, *Children Eating Grapes and a Melon*, c. 1645. Oil on canvas, 145.9 × 103.6 cm (605), Alte Pinakothek, Munich. Image courtesy of incamerastock / Alamy Stock Photo.

formula in particular, 'children deny, or enable us to forget, many aspects of adult society'.[56] Hence, as class identity re-emerges in the nineteenth-century sentimental picture – though it was previously ubiquitous, as Murillo's example confirms – this alone cannot be the culprit for the emotionality particular to this new type of painting. Instead, what is at stake must be the way in which emotions are rendered in these pictures.

Now, returning to the issue of pictorial aesthetics, art historian Ragni Linnet has put forward the theory that an idealization took hold in the late Danish Golden Age painting from the 1840s onwards. Kasper Monrad suggests something similar, emphasizing that allegory, which was otherwise rarely a part of everyday

56 Higonnet, *Pictures of Innocence*, 23.

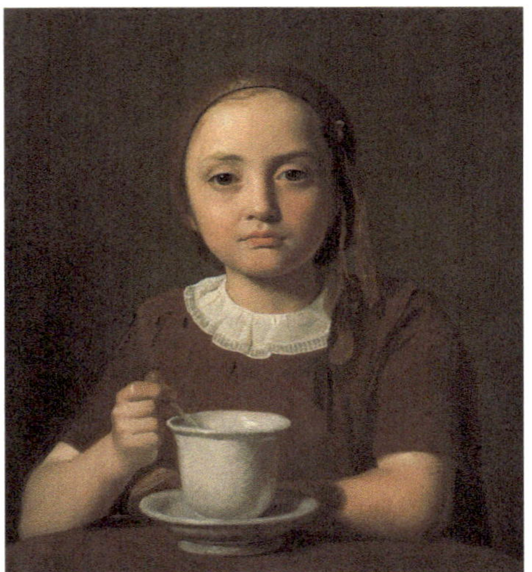

Figure 21. Constantin Hansen, *Portrait of a Little Girl, Elise Købke, with a Cup in front of her*, 1850. Oil on paper, 39 cm × 35.5 cm (KMS3388), The National Gallery of Denmark, Copenhagen. Image courtesy of the National Gallery of Denmark.

scenes, emerged with renewed force in a number of ambitious canvases.[57] Both observers take Hansen's small portrait study of *Portrait of a Little Girl, Elise Købke, with a Cup in front of her* (1850, National Gallery of Denmark, fig. 21) as evidence for their theses. Here, the girl sits motionless and expressionless in front of a large cup, which she stirs, were it not for the impression of a stiffened gesture. Linnet highlights not only the stylization but also the iconographic gulf that separates the girl's portrait from Christian Albrecht Jensen's portrait art from twenty years earlier.[58] Conversely, discussing a similar, – even later – children's portrait by Hansen, art historian David Jackson centres on 'how Danish artists were drawn to directness and integrity in their observations', thus perpetuating the standard narrative in Danish Golden Age scholarship.[59] Whether one agrees or disagrees with Linnet's approach, which is indebted to the history of ideas, her explanatory model is also applicable to Schleisner's and Larsen's strategic simplification and statuary isolation, only the end goal here is different, namely the sentimental response. Since probably not all painters had an actual poetics, as Monrad credits Hansen with, one could speculate whether the growth and

57 Monrad, *Hverdagsbilleder*, 277–279; Ragni Linnet, "Guldalderens billedudtryk i filosofisk optik", *Meddelelser fra Thorvaldsen's Museum* (1994).

58 Linnet, "Guldalderens billedudtryk i filosofisk optik", 27–28.

59 Jackson, *Danish Golden Age Painting*, 127.

stabilization of the art market have something to say in this regard.[60] But here, it must remain a thought.

The Outsider Elisabeth Jerichau Baumann

Finally, it can be beneficial to juxtapose the previous examples with a study of a painter who strictly speaking does not belong to the Danish Golden Age, considering her educational background, namely Elisabeth Jerichau Baumann (1818–1881). She was not a student of the Danish Academy of Fine Arts but of the Düsseldorf Art Academy, which became famous and notorious for promoting and disseminating a polished, detailed academic painting style in dark tones. She never gained great recognition in Copenhagen's art scene, but considering that she, all things considered, had a large clientele among the royal family and nobility, and that she also chose Danish motifs, it seems reasonable to include her here.[61] Likewise, her popularity in England makes her an interesting nomadic artist.

Jerichau Baumann's efforts span a wide range of motifs, with portraits in particular playing a leading role. However, her comeback in recent years has primarily been driven by a fascination with her Orientalist depictions. But portrait and genre painting also constitute a large part of her output. As we have established, it was Greuze's scene with a Bible reading in a peasant home that heralded the sentimental wave in genre painting. Jerichau Baumann built her reputation on just such a motif (now with a Danish rural atmosphere), *Devotional Scene*, which was even executed in nine versions, the largest of which (1860, private collection, fig. 22) was commissioned by Napoleon III.[62] Here we see the parents' moved reaction to the daughter's Bible reading, placing the work type in the early sentimental – and less assertive – paradigm in the spirit of Greuze.

Her artistic career was also supported by the Danish royal family. King Christian IX and Queen Louise, for example, bought *A Little Flower Girl* (1857, Christiansborg Palace, exhibited at Charlottenborg in 1858, fig. 23).[63] Here, a small, blond girl with a red cap and large, blue eyes looks directly at the viewer, holding a large bouquet of mixed summer flowers in her arms. The background is brown, matte, and monotonous. The picture type, where only the head is in focus,

60 Monrad, *Hverdagsbilleder*, 279.

61 Sine Krogh, "The Phenomenal Elisabeth Jerichau-Baumann", in *Elisabeth Jerichau-Baumann: Mellem verdener / Between Worlds*, ed. Erlend G. Høyersten, Anne Mette Thomsen, and Jakob Vengberg Sevel (Aarhus: ARoS Aarhus Kunstmuseum, 2021), 39–43.

62 Jerzy Miskowiak, *Elisabeth Jerichau-Baumann: Nationalromantikkens enfant terrible – en værkoversigt* (Frederiksberg: Frydenlund, 2018), 220–223.

63 Miskowiak, *Elisabeth Jerichau-Baumann*, 229.

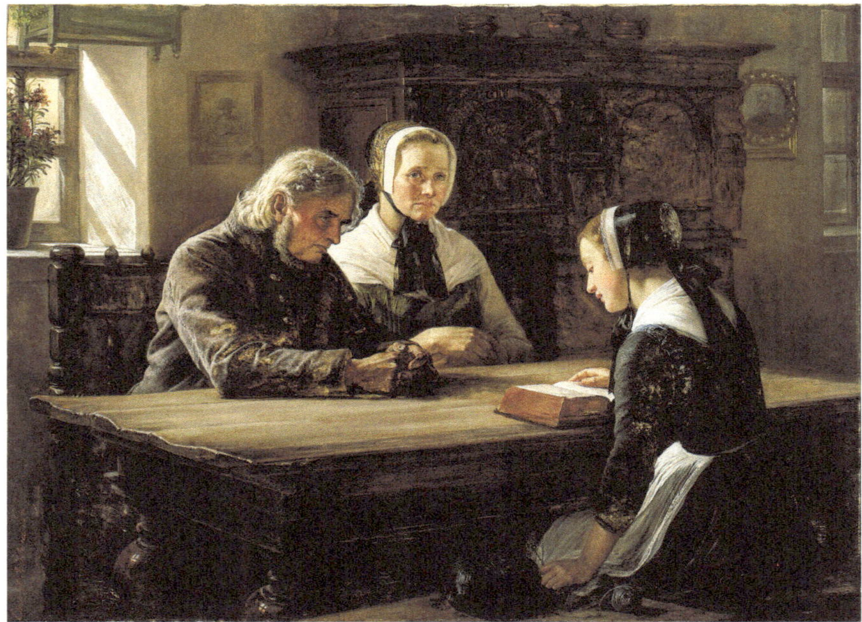

Figure 22. Elisabeth Jerichau Baumann, *Devotional Scene*, 1860. Oil on canvas, 144 cm × 192 cm, private collection. Image courtesy of Jerzy Miskowiak.

and the background is summarily suggested – a modern figurehead or *tronie* – is one of Jerichau Baumann's archetypes, and it recurs across cultures. Not only is her approach vastly different from, say, Frans Hals (1582–1666) two centuries before, as is any Danish Golden Age figure study; she also renews the repertoire in a new, more expansive, spirit of sentimentality, which a comparison with Hansen's *Portrait of a Little Girl* will immediately reveal. In keeping with his Eckersbergian outlook on the creative process as a process of filtering out any superfluous and distracting detail in order to convey a refined reality, Hansen's picture announces the formalist conditions of its own making.[64]

In Jerichau Baumann's portrayal, the girl's head, with its wide-open eyes and direct gaze distinguishing it from the 'Greuze girl', is characterized as a Gypsy and in Danish, Turkish, Italian, Jewish, and many other regional or ethnic variants. This applies to *A Little Girl from Amager* (1865, private collection), *A Girl in Regional Costume* (1879, private collection), *La pensierosa (The Thoughtful One)* (1875, private collection), *An Italian Girl with a Cherry as an Earring* (1878, private collection), and *A Young Turkish Woman Sends a Carrier Pigeon to her Chosen One* (c. 1870, private collection). Beggary or street vending is often

64 Monrad, *Hverdagsbilleder*, 279.

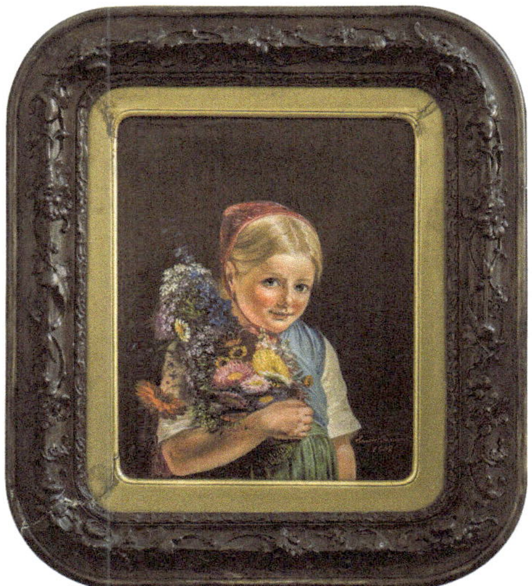

Figure 23. Elisabeth Jerichau Baumann, *A Little Flower Girl*, 1857. Oil on canvas, 27 cm × 21 cm, Christiansborg Palace, Copenhagen. Image courtesy of The Danish Royal Family. Photographer: Berit Møller, The Royal Danish Collection.

included in the motif, as in *Roman Children Selling Violets* (date unknown, private collection), making the direct gaze into a request to the viewer. In most cases, however, the gaze does not carry a clear emotion but becomes a pure relation of address and thus an empty gesture.

Nevertheless, Jerichau Baumann's direct practice is fundamentally different from even Greuze's popular girls' heads, whose eyes hardly ever look out at the viewer. Instead, the eyes are turned skyward, dreamy, and generally directed towards places outside the picture zone. The effect often leads to an air of self-forgetfulness, as mentioned earlier, but Greuze's direct model is religious paintings of devoted female saints.

In addition, Jerichau Baumann systematically enlarges the girls' eyes in relation to the size of the face beyond the average norm.[65] Psychologist Andrew S. Winston, in his study of sentimental painting, has found that larger eyes give subjects the impression that the portrayed person possesses 'physical weakness, intellectual naivety, social submissiveness, warmth, honesty, and kindness', which gives the impression of 'an overall characteristic of babyness in a human face'.[66]

65 This is also typical of cartoon characters whose traits are derived from 'cute' animals, see: Steven Jay Gould, "A Biological Homage to Mickey Mouse", *The Panda's Thumb: More Reflections in Natural History* (New York: W. W. Norton & Co., 1980), 95–107.

66 Andrew S. Winston, "Sweetness and light: Psychological aesthetics and sentimental art", in

Where a close or unexpected cropping in the early Golden Age paintings sharpens the feeling of intimacy and proximity to the experienced scene, Jerichau Baumann's zoom effect instead serves to heighten the pure emotional intensity and impact. This leads partly to the state of addressing an imaginary viewer, as Lyons concretizes by another example, and partly to a subordination of the picture's other means to the pure expressive signalling via the face.

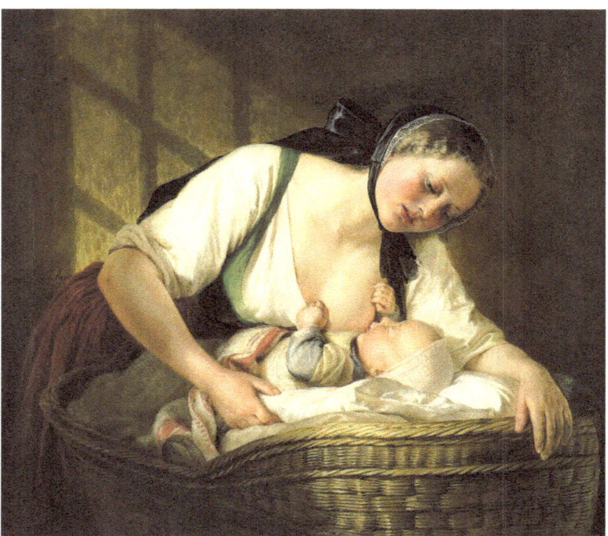

Figure 24. Elisabeth Jerichau Baumann, *A Mother with Her Child*, 1852. Oil on canvas, 82 cm × 92 cm, private collection. Image courtesy of Wikimedia Commons.

Motherhood occupies a significant place in Jerichau Baumann's oeuvre, and unlike her overwhelmingly male competitors, she was familiar with the role of motherhood. Therefore, it is to be expected that her depictions of motherhood would deviate from the stereotypical and idealized, often italianizing, image type practised by many Danish Golden Age painters and preserved, for instance, in the contemporaneous and representative Thorvaldsen's Museum collection. Motherhood's lot is depicted here with tenderness and sweetness but also as an extremely passive affair. Or, as Eaton writes, with a caricatured emotional life:

> Typically, these are tied to the general sins of deceptiveness or misplaced or undue idealism, to children who are thoroughly innocent or women who perform no bodily functions other than weeping, fainting or blushing, for example.[67]

Emerging visions of the aesthetic process: Psychology, semiology, and philosophy, ed. Gerald C. Cupchik and János László (Cambridge: Cambridge University Press, 1992), 124.

67 Eaton, "Laughing at the Death of Little Nell", 274.

However, that is not the case. Jerichau Baumann's maternal images are characterized by the placeless sentimentality, embellishment, and idealization, just as she opts out of the secondary figures that could further characterize the scene (such as the maids seen in a typical Dutch genre painting, or even in almost every motherhood scene by Marguerite Gérard (1761–1837)). A comparison of Jerichau Baumann's *A Mother with Her Child* (1852, private collection, fig. 24) with Gérard's *La mère nourrice (The Nourishing Mother)* (1804, Clark Art Institute, also known as *Les premiers pas / The First Steps*, fig. 25) will suffice as an example.[68] Once again, one must resort to a potential mapping of the art market, as well as to her global nomadic existence, as keys to explanation, but this lies beyond the scope of this article.

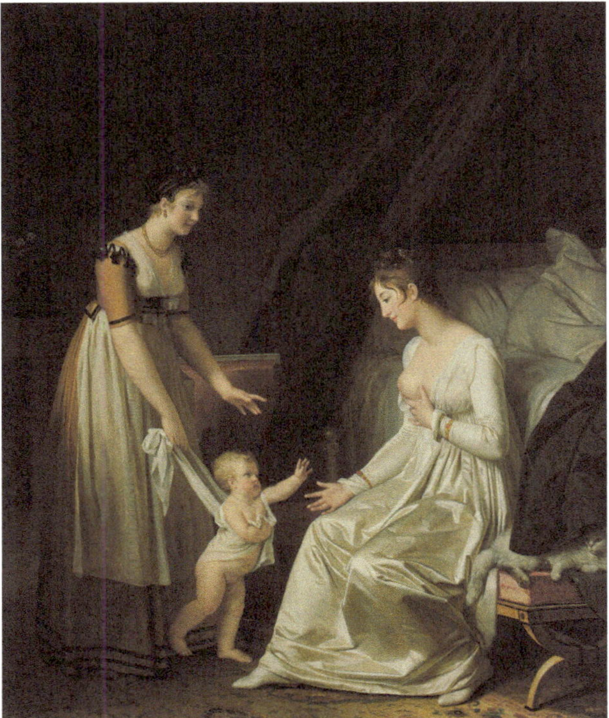

Figure 25. Marguerite Gérard, *La mère nourrice (The Nourishing Mother)*, 1804. Oil on canvas, 60.5 cm × 50 cm (2022.16), Clark Art Institute, Williamstown, Massachusetts. Image courtesy of Clark Art Institute.

68 An earlier, yet similarly sized version exists in the holdings of Villa Musée Jean-Honoré Fragonard in Grasse.

Conclusion and Discussion

In his groundbreaking text on the Dutch group portrait, Alois Riegl observes that the Dutch succeeded more than any others before them in cultivating attention (*Aufmerksamkeit*) as an implicit principle of figural painting:

> Dutch painting would construct a bridge between figures through the representation of a selfless psychological element (attention), by means of which the individual psyches were forged together as a whole in the consciousness of the beholding subject.[69]

For Riegl, the group portrait represented an arena where a modern painterly problem – allowing the individual to stand out in a collective without compromising the whole – was first identified. Rembrandt's (1606–1669) ongoing contributions to the genre were, for Riegl, superior attempts at solving this dilemma because the mutual attention between the figures both preserved psychological individuality and unified the composition. As we have seen, this attention can also extend to depictions of children, both portraits and genre pieces, in the early Danish Golden Age from the 1820s and 1830s.

Supplementing this with Fried, Greuze appears to address another modern painterly problem, the relationship between absorption and theatricality. Additionally, there is the issue of sentimentality. For both Fried and Vanpée, however, Greuze's innovation does not diminish the viewer's role in completing the picture as an image. Fried emphasizes the imagined emotional life cultivated by the girl turning her back on everyday life, while Vanpée focuses on the erotic fantasy accessed by deciphering the painting's code language and going beyond the immediate surface. The centrifugal gaze of the 'Greuze girl' serves to make the girl's thoughts inscrutable and inaccessible to the viewer.

A similar appeal to the imagination of the beholder is not found in the sentimental pictures of Larsen, Schleisner, Schack, or Jerichau Baumann. Formally, they present static or even statuesque figures placed in placeless environments without topographical or other distinct features. Facial expressions and gestures are deliberately limited or subdued. Body language may be uneven, prioritizing the face over the rest of the body, with eyes disproportionately exaggerated at the expense of the rest of the face. Due to the static body language and the general preference for depicting a state rather than an action, there are no significant motifs of movement with which the viewer can identify phenomenologically or react to. Our ability, through the imagination, to complete a sequence of actions or a logical progression is therefore limited or impossible. Emotionally, there are passive states of despair, powerlessness, sadness, and similarly passive ex-

69 Aloïs Riegl and Benjamin Binstock, trans., "Excerpts from *The Dutch Group Portrait*" [1902], *October* 74 (Autumn, 1995): 11. https://doi.org/10.2307/778818.

pressions of joy, where the source of the smile (if relevant) can only be the viewer himself or herself, not events within the picture itself. Thus, we as beholders are construed as triggers of the children's attention, and the voyeurism characteristic of the construction of the 'Greuze girl' disappears in favour of an unmistakable staging of the viewer as the object and main interest of the gaze. All remnants of absorption disappear simultaneously and are replaced by calculated theatricality. Events are portrayed with diffuse reactions, often in the form of anxiety or worry, which do not match the depicted or alluded-to looming threat, thus adhering to the common definition of sentimentality as a misplaced, exaggerated emotional response.

Triggered by a curiosity about the explosion in art historical literature about individual artworks over the past century, James Elkins asks, *Why Are Our Pictures Puzzles?* Giorgio Vasari could describe a work of art in just a few lines in the sixteenth century, while today it requires several books. Elkins' answer – that art history overcomplicates works of art to have something to write about – is provocative, but we must take stock of the diagnosis he presents. Despite his convincing argument that much of the supposed complexity in images is self-created, the previous analyses suggest that the Danish sentimental Golden Age paintings are not difficult to understand and, in some respects, they are lacking in compositional complexity when compared to their earlier Dutch and Danish forebears. As I have tentatively suggested, both the works by De Bray, Netscher, and Steen of the Dutch School and the works by Jensen, Hansen, and Marstrand of the Danish School – all depicting children – bear the imprint of internal compositional connectivity achieved either by gaze or gesture. Furthermore, under certain circumstances, this connectivity has the potential of inducing in the beholder a certain curiosity or mystification, as Fried's notion of absorption suggests. In any case, the type of attention between individuals, identified by Riegl, disappears as a compositional strategy in the directness of later Golden Age sentimental pictures.

In her studies of Victorian sentimental culture, Pamela Fletcher seeks to define a historical understanding of what viewers in the nineteenth century expected from a genre painting. For this purpose, she consulted contemporary art reviews, which reveal that both immoral content – such as infidelity – and emotional excesses, especially of a contemporary nature – such as a massacre – exceeded good taste, so artists sought to create images that could evoke a diffuse emotional sensitivity – that is, works 'full of "genuine emotion" or filled with "human feeling"'.[70] Specific emotions are rarely elaborated in this art criticism,

70 Pamela Fletcher, "Tender Beauty: Victorian Painting and the Problem of Sentimentality", *Journal of Victorian Culture* 16, no. 2 (2011): 462. https://doi.org/10.1080/13555502.2011.589678.

writes Fletcher. She wonders if the Victorians were deceiving themselves when they stressed how genre painting should ideally emphasize *empathy* but, in reality, created a visual culture with *sympathy* as visual currency. Duncum's choice of wording supports this conclusion.[71] Unlike empathy, where one feels another's pain or distress, sympathy only calls for recognition, not necessarily action or intervention. Empathy is kept in moderation, and the distance between the artwork and the viewer is thus intact.[72] Thus, the emotional effect of sympathy in fact mitigates the directness of the gaze confronting the beholder so typical of sentimental genre paintings.

A similar conclusion, drawn through different means, can also be applied to the late Danish Golden Age sentimental genre painting. When Linnet and Monrad find that the late Golden Age is fundamentally different from its earlier phase, their findings can be corroborated by fundamental shifts in compositional preference. In the most extreme cases, this shift surfaces as a channelling of all available emotional energy into facial expression at the expense of preserving the wholeness of bodily communication.[73] This strategy, in terms of the intensity of emotional appeal, almost pre-empts the later fragmentation seen in modern painting. However, in terms of the picture serving as a pure vehicle for emotional recognition rather than a formal statement, it runs counter to the formalist impulses in modern painting, at least.

71 'For such children, the nineteenth-century middle class could enjoy the pleasant sensation of sympathy.' Duncum, *Images of Childhood*, 29.

72 Fletcher, "Tender Beauty", 468.

73 Likewise, the humour is coarser in the earlier period's genre painting than in the later times, but that is another story. See: Jesper Svenningsen, "From obscure wit to popular jokes: Humour in 1820s and 1830s painting", in *Danish Golden Age – World-class art between disasters*, ed. Cecilie Høgsbro Østergaard (Copenhagen: The National Gallery of Denmark, 2019).

Anna Bohlin
(University of Bergen)

Figures of Emancipation: Organicist Imagery between Romanticism and Darwinism

Abstract

Feminist theory in the early twentieth century built on a tradition of feminist thought in literature. I use linguistic theories of the metaphor to argue that the imagery in the Nordic emancipation novels of the 1850s may be studied as a theorization of women's emancipation, and that the shift of theoretical underpinning during the second half of the nineteenth century may be traced in the transformation of a romantic, organicist imagery. The first part of the analysis shows how the organicist metaphors in Collett's *Amtmandens Døttre* (1854–1855), Fibiger's *Clara Raphael* (1851), Bremer's *Hertha* (1856), and Runeberg's *Fru Catharina Boije och hennes döttrar* (1858) conceive of women's rights within a romantic understanding of *Bildung* in connection to a Christian notion of evolution. The second part of the analysis highlights the displacement of the organicist metaphors towards an imagery associated with evolutionary biology in Collett's collections of essays of the 1870s.

Keywords

Camilla Collett, women's emancipation, deliberate metaphors, organicism, Nordic emancipation novels

In Camilla Collett's grand essay on women's emancipation "Om Kvinden og hendes Stilling" (On the woman and her position) from 1872, she envisioned women's emancipation to be spread like 'Blomsterstøvet med Vinden, usynlig, ufattelig, og med uimodstaaelig Magt vil den gribe Alle' (pollen carried by the wind, invisible, incomprehensible, and with irresistible power, it will capture everyone).[1] Imagining emancipation in terms of pollination could only have happened at precisely this point in history. At the inception of the nineteenth century, the notion that women's rights might fill the air would have been in-

1 Camilla Collett, "Om Kvinden og hendes Stilling" in *Sidste Blade. Erindringer og Bekjendelser. Anden og tredie Række* (Christiania: P. L. Malling, 1872), 55–115, quotation on p. 60. I would like to thank the research group of Nordic literature at the University of Bergen for useful comments on an earlier draft of this article and especially Helga Mannsåker for suggesting linguistic theories of the metaphor and Helen Leslie for proofreading. I'm also grateful for important remarks in the anonymous peer review.

conceivable, and a few decades later, the vaporized nature of that simile would most likely have seemed too intangible, possibly even too romantic. Emancipation as pollination would not even have been viable in Collett's own emancipation novel, *Amtmandens Døttre* (published in English as *The District Governor's Daughters),* issued less than twenty years earlier in 1854–1855 – and not, for that matter, in any of the other Nordic emancipation novels issued in the 1850s. Collett is often presented as being alone in her struggle for women's rights.[2] However, from a Nordic perspective she was not alone: *The District Governor's Daughters* was preceded by the Danish Mathilde Fibiger's *Clara Raphael. Tolv Breve* (Clara Raphael: twelve letters) issued in 1851 and followed by the Swedish Fredrika Bremer's *Hertha* in 1856, and the Finnish Fredrika Runeberg's *Fru Catharina Boije och hennes döttrar. En berättelse från stora ofredens tid* (Lady Catharina Boije and her daughters: a story from the time of the greater wrath), from 1858. The flower imagery is indeed abundant in all these novels; in fact, organicist metaphors carry the arguments for women's liberation. However, during the second half of the nineteenth century, the organicist imagery would change – as would the theoretical underpinning of women's rights. Collett's authorship, covering most of the second part of the nineteenth century, provides an opportunity for examining that displacement.

The modern struggle for women's rights is usually dated back to the French Revolution. During the nineteenth century, the understanding of the driving forces of emancipation was displaced from a romantic conception of *Bildung* to Darwinist evolutionary biology. It is well known that emancipation in feminist theory at the beginning of the twentieth century was generally conceived of within an 'evolutionistic frame of reference', as Sylvia Määttä has put it.[3] Darwinism, and other kinds of evolutionary biology, had become the general theory of the day, and even though it was often used for misogynist purposes, feminists were not slow in claiming evolutionist thoughts for their own ends, stating that women's emancipation should be considered a law of nature.[4] To be sure, Collett never

2 See for example Kristin Ørjasæter, *Camilla: Norges første feminist* (Oslo: Cappelen, 2003), 152; Ellisiv Steen, *Den lange strid: Camilla Collett og hennes senere forfatterskap* (Oslo: Gyldendal norsk forlag, 1954), 269.

3 Sylvia Määttä, *Kön och evolution: Charlotte Perkins Gilmans feministiska utopier 1911–1916* (diss. Göteborg: Bokförlaget Nya Doxa, 1997), 2, 51.

4 See for example Sally Ledger, *The New Woman: Fiction and feminism at the fin de siècle* (Manchester and New York: Manchester University Press, 1997); Carolyn Burdett, *Olive Schreiner and the Progress of Feminism: Evolution, Gender, Empire* (Basingstoke and New York: Palgrave, 2001); Anna Bohlin, *Röstens anatomi. Läsningar av politik i Elin Wägners* Silverforsen, *Selma Lagerlöfs Löwensköldtrilogi och Klara Johansons Tidevarvskåserier* (diss. Umeå: Bokförlaget h:ström, 2008); Cecilia Annell, *Begärets politiska potential. Feministiska motståndsstrategier i Elin Wägners* Pennskaftet, *Gabriele Reuters* Aus guter Familie, *Hilma Angered-Strandbergs* Lydia Vik *och Grete Meisel-Hess* Die Intellektuellen (diss. Södertörn, Lund: Ellerström, 2016).

became a Darwinist. Still, she became a great inspiration to someone who did. The controversial Swedish feminist Ellen Key (1849–1926) would become one of the leading theorists to introduce Darwinist evolutionism to feminist theory. In her very first published article, she took her cue from Collett in her comparison of human societies to animals.[5]

The aim of this article is to analyze how organicist imagery carried the arguments for women's rights and worked as a theoretical underpinning of women's emancipation in the Nordic emancipation novels of the 1850s. Furthermore, a few examples drawn from Collett's essays of the 1870s will suggest how the imagery in arguments for women's rights display an increasing affinity with the evolutionist frame of reference that would come to govern feminist thought at the turn of the twentieth century. The displacement of organicist metaphors in Collett's authorship will serve as a case study to highlight the shift in feminist thought and to recognize the theoretical, as well as argumentative, value of metaphors in exploring that shift.

Feminist theory, established as a genre at the turn of the twentieth century, built on a tradition of feminist thought in literature. In the novel, political arguments rest not exclusively on explicit political demands; they are rather embedded in the composition and, perhaps even more importantly, in the figuration employed in the novel. The linguistic 'theory of conceptual metaphor' draws attention to the explanatory function of metaphors. The metaphor, they point out, is conceptual in nature: 'metaphor is not simply a matter of words or linguistic expressions but of concepts, of thinking of one thing in terms of another'.[6] Conceptual metaphors are essential components in cognitive models, and plants and human bodies are indeed favoured 'source domains' – or *topoi*, as a literary historian would have it – to make sense of complex abstract systems. Certain properties are thus transferred from the 'source domain' to the 'target domain'.[7] In that respect, figuration is theorization; it suggests a cognitive model to make sense of, for example, women's emancipation.

The linguist Lotte van Poppel has discussed the communicative dimension of metaphors in argumentation. She uses the term 'deliberate metaphor' for metaphors 'intended to change the perspective on the target domain', for example in

5 Ellen Key, "Camille Collet [sic] och hennes författareverksamhet," *Tidskrift för hemmet* 16, no. 5 (1874) 262–77. See also Anna Bohlin, "Camilla Collett – den felande länken i svensk litteraturhistoria" in *Med kärlek: En festskrift till Claudia Lindén*, eds. Eva Jonsson, Ann-Sofie Lönngren, Mattias Pirholt, and Oscar von Seth (Huddinge: Södertörns högskola, 2023), 41–65.

6 The theory of conceptual metaphor was launched in 1980 by George Lakoff and Mark Johnson. Zoltán Kövecses, *Metaphor: A Practical Introduction* (Oxford: Oxford University Press, 2010), x–xi, 4–10.

7 Kövecses, *Metaphor,* 126–32, 155–62.

order 'to change someone's opinion'.[8] Thus, van Poppel writes, they also have 'an argumentative function' in 'resolving the difference of opinion'.[9] Obviously, not all metaphors are to be considered deliberate in this sense – in fact most uses of metaphors are non-deliberate, but deliberate metaphors, she states, 'may be regarded as relevant argumentative moves'.[10] As this analysis will show, the organicist metaphors appear at pivotal moments in the Nordic emancipation novels of the 1850s and as key points in Collett's essays. The figuration used to convey emancipation provides a frame of reference, legitimization, and explanation, a key for interpreting foundational concepts, and above all to argue for women's rights. The metaphors have indeed an argumentative function and reflect changing ideas and theoretical standpoints. That also applies to a pamphlet like Mary Wollstonecraft's *A Vindication of the Rights of Woman* (1792).

In the following, Mary Wollstonecraft's *A Vindication of the Rights of Woman* will provide a point of reference for early feminist discourse, formulated in direct response to the French Revolution, and couched in Enlightenment rhetoric and incipient romantic thought. My argument concerning the use of flower imagery in Collett's *The District Governor's Daughters* will be corroborated by a Nordic context. The first part of the analysis will investigate organicist imagery in the Nordic emancipation novels of the 1850s. Camilla Collett (1813–1895), Mathilde Fibiger (1830–1872), Fredrika Bremer (1801–1865), and Fredrika Runeberg (1807–1879) all shared an aesthetics that invited realism, although firmly rooted in romanticism. In fact, Bremer published the first indigenous bourgeois realist novel in Sweden, *Familien H**** (1830–1831).[11] Fibiger's *Clara Raphael* gives a realist account of bourgeois life in a small country town, but her romantic conception of women and of love was too idealist even for many of her contemporaries. The heroine solves the conflict between emancipation and desire with an asexual marriage, which caused quite a stir.[12] Runeberg's historical novel

8 The definition reads: 'intentionally used as metaphors between sender and addressee to invite interlocutors to view the target domain in terms of the source domain'. Lotte van Poppel, "The Relevance of Metaphor in Argumentation: Uniting Pragma-dialectics and Deliberate Metaphor Theory," *Journal of Pragmatics* 170 (2020), 245–52, quotations on p. 246–47.

9 van Poppel, 249.

10 van Poppel, 251.

11 For a discussion on Bremer's aesthetics, see Birgitta Holm, *Romanens mödrar 1: Fredrika Bremer och den borgerliga romanens födelse* (Stockholm: P.A. Norstedt & Söner Förlag, 1981); Åsa Arping, *Den anspråksfulla blygsamheten. Auktoritet och genus i 1830-talets svenska romandebatt* (Eslöv: Symposion, 2002).

12 Katalin Nun, *Women of the Danish Golden Age: Literature, Theater and the Emancipation of Women* (Copenhagen: Museum Tusculanum Press, 2013), 85–129; Stig Dalager and Anne-Marie Mai, *Danske kvindelige forfattere I – fra Sophie Brahe til Mathilde Fibiger. Udvikling og perspektiv* (Copenhagen: Gyldendal, 1982). On the debate on Fibiger's novel, see Marius Wulfsberg, "Kvinnefrigjøring og offentlighet i Norden på 1850-tallet. Om Mathilde Fibigers *Clara Raphael* og Camilla Colletts *Amtmandens Døttre*" in *Frie ord i Norden? Offentlighet,*

Fru Catharina Boije och hennes döttrar, set during the Great Northern War in the early eighteenth century, was written in the 1840s (and therefore strictly speaking the first of the Nordic emancipation novels), but not published until 1858. Thorough research ensured accurate historical details, but the historical events are embedded in a romance plot; Runeberg's ideas on femininity and love were indisputably romantic.[13] In Norwegian literary history, Collett's novel often marks the transition from romanticism to realism.[14] Kristin Ørjasæter has stressed the importance of the romantic concept of love in Collett's novel, that is, erotic love as a gateway to embrace the love of God.[15] However, for the third edition issued in 1879, Collett made substantial changes to align the novel with the contemporary realist paradigm.[16] All the Nordic emancipation novels of the 1850s used organicist imagery as conceptual and deliberate, argumentative metaphors for women's emancipation. The plant imagery remained active in Collett's later essays, but the significance would be altered as the century drew to its end.

The second part of the analysis will trace the displacement of the organicist imagery in Collett's collections of essays, issued in 1868–1885. Whereas Bremer died in 1865 and Fibiger's and Runeberg's literary production was scant after the 1860s, Collett's long life and prolific output of essays provide an excellent ex-

ytringsfrihet og medborgerskap 1814–1914, eds. Ruth Hemstad and Dag Michalsen (Oslo: Pax Forlag, 2019), 411–34.

13 Heidi Grönstrand, "Historical Fiction and the Dynamics of Romance: The Cases of Evald Ferdinand Jahnsson and Fredrika Runeberg" in *Novels, Histories, Novel Nations: Historical Fiction and Cultural Memory in Finland and Estonia*, eds. Linda Kaljundi, Eneken Laanes, and Ilona Pikkanen (Helsinki: Finnish Literature Society, 2015), 140–56; Pia Forssell, "Fredrika Runeberg mellan familjeideologi och emancipation" in *Festskrift till Johan Wrede*, ed. Magnus Pettersson (Helsingfors: Svenska litteratursällskapet i Finland, 1995), 105–12; Merete Mazzarella, *Fredrika Charlotta född Tengström. En nationalskalds hustru* (Helsinki: Svenska litteratursällskapet i Finland & Stockholm: Atlantis, 2007).

14 Ellisiv Steen, *Diktning og virkelighet: En studie i Camilla Colletts forfatterskap* (Oslo: Gyldendal norsk forlag, 1947), 90–91, 122–23, 283–85; Steen, *Den lange strid: Camilla Collett og hennes senere forfatterskap*, 260–68.

15 Kristin Ørjasæter, "Camilla Colletts kristne feminisme" in *Å bli en stemme: Nye studier i Camilla Colletts forfatterskap*, ed. Trond Haugen (Oslo: Novus, 2014), 153–72, see esp. p. 158; Ørjasæter, *Camilla: Norges første feminist*, 17–25. See also Toril Moi, "Stumhet og kjærlighed: En lesning av Amtmandens Døttre" in *Å bli en stemme: Nye studier i Camilla Colletts forfatterskap*, ed. Trond Haugen (Oslo: Novus, 2014), 33–55. Erik Bjerck Hagen, on the other hand, states that 'Camilla Collett's romanticism was always realist'. Erik Bjerck Hagen, *Norsk litteratur 1830–1875: Romantikk, realisme, modernisme* (Oslo: Dreyer, 2019), 250–51, my translation. On the influence from German romanticism and connections to 'das junge Deutschland', see also Torill Steinfeld, *Camilla Collett: Ungdom og ekteskap* (Oslo: Gyldendal Norsk Forlag, 2012), 230–39, 267–85.

16 Moi, "Stumhet og kjærlighet", 40; Ørjasæter, *Camilla: Norges første feminist,* 99; Kristin Ørjasæter, "Innledning" in Camilla Collett, *Amtmandens Døttre*, eds. Ellen Nessheim & Kristin Ørjasæter, digital edition, (Det norske spark- og litteratursellskap, 2013); Steen, *Den lange strid: Camilla Collett og hennes senere forfatterskap*, 267–68.

ample with which to explore the conceptual and argumentative metaphors used in the transition between romanticism and Darwinism. Before embarking upon the analysis, a brief introduction to romantic organicism is in order.

Organicism, Bildung, bloom

The concepts 'organism' and 'evolution' that seem self-evident to us today had a long and complex history before they were stabilized at the beginning of the nineteenth century. For centuries, the secret of life was to be found at its inception, the task was to explain the origin of the shape of organs. Historian Elías Palti has studied the process leading to the romantic concept of the organism, and highlights that most of the earlier theories subscribed in different ways to so-called 'preformationism', meaning 'that all features of adult organisms were already fully perceivable in the embryo from its conception'.[17] However, the shift away from preformationism should not be understood as a shift away from God as the omnipotent creator.[18] The Christian notion of evolution was a powerful model to make sense of cultural and natural history, even after the publication of Charles Darwin's *On the Origin of Species* in 1859.[19] Conversely, as Peter J. Bowler has stressed, Darwin's study was preceded by earlier theories that included humanity in the evolution of the natural world, and the Darwinian version of evolution theory remained controversial long after its publication.[20]

How to come to terms with progress and Man's place in the organic world was indeed a central and contested issue throughout the nineteenth century. The prerequisite for that debate was that new scientific ideas at the end of the eighteenth century, in Palti's words, 'began to incorporate teleological processes within the reach of reason'; the future was found to be inherent in materiality.[21] He stresses the importance of the shift from causal to finalistic-holistic explanations of life, 'the organism'. The study of organs no longer looked for the origin but

17 Elías Palti, "Romantic Philosophy and Natural Sciences: Blurred Boundaries and Terminological Problems," *Contributions to the History of Concepts* 1, no. 1 (March 2005), 83–108, quotation on p. 83–84. See also Denise Gigante, *Life: Organic Form and Romanticism* (New Haven & London: Yale University Press, 2009), 7–23.

18 Palti, "Romantic Philosophy and Natural Sciences"; Gigante, *Life*, 7–9.

19 See for example *Tracing the Jerusalem Code. Volume 3. The Promised Land: Christian Cultures in Modern Scandinavia (ca. 1750–ca. 1920)*, eds. Ragnhild J. Zorgati and Anna Bohlin (Berlin: De Gruyter, 2021).

20 Peter J. Bowler, *Theories of Human Evolution: A Century of Debate, 1844–1944* (Oxford: Basil Blackwell, 1987), 2, 42.

21 Palti, "Romantic Philosophy and Natural Sciences," 93.

rather for the *function* in the reproduction of the organism.[22] Growth, instead of origin, would become the main centre of attention.

Growth is the key to both *organicism* and *Bildung,* two central concepts in romantic aestheticism and philosophy. Philosopher Frederick C. Beiser emphasises, in his study *The Romantic Imperative*, the romantics' belief in 'organic unity' in connection to their 'fundamental goal: *Bildung*, the education of humanity, the development of all human powers into a whole'.[23] *Bildung*, Beiser explains, signifies two mutually interdependent processes: 'learning and personal growth'.[24] Freedom is the guiding principle; Beiser quotes Friedrich Schlegel's definition of *Bildung* as '"the development of independence" (*Entwicklung der Selbständigkeit*)'.[25] Literary historian Denise Gigante reminds us that *Bildung* conflates biology and aesthetics, as it initially was a physiological concept.[26] She points out that Friedrich Schiller made use of his training in physiology when he argued for the vital importance of aesthetic education for societal change based on an organic model: aesthetics 'could reanimate and regenerate the world'.[27] In Shiller's *Über die ästhetische Erziehung des Menschen* (1795), he understood the living form to be '*inherently* political', Gigante writes.[28] True political freedom must be the result of an inner freedom cultivated by aesthetic taste, harmony, and beauty – in short, of *Bildung.* That idea of freedom was a major inspiration for mid-nineteenth-century thought on women's emancipation.[29] The fundamentally political nature of the romantic concepts of *Bildung* and organic growth is the reason why women's rights were conceived of in terms of organisms, of plants and bodies. It also specified the interconnection between individual growth and the progress of society.

22 Preformation and evolution had 'in the context of the Enlightenment's universe of ideas [been] mutually contradictory', but they were now reconciled, yet not until 1828 in Karl E. von Baer, in *Über Entwickelungsgeschichte der Thiere.* Palti, "Romantic Philosophy and Natural Sciences," 83–85, 95, 103. See also Gigante, *Life*, 7–23.

23 Frederick C. Beiser, *The Romantic Imperative: The Concept of Early German Romanticism* (Cambridge, Massachusetts, & London: Harvard University Press: 2003), 22, 97.

24 Beiser, *The Romantic Imperative,* 91.

25 Friedrich Schlegel quoted in Beiser, *The Romantic Imperative*, 100.

26 Gigante, *Life*, 46.

27 Gigante, *Life*, 26.

28 Gigante, *Life*, 25. See also Beiser, *The Romantic Imperative*, 93–103.

29 Historian Anne-Lise Seip discusses the impact of Schiller's concept of freedom on the Norwegian national poet Johan Sebastian Welhaven. Even though Camilla Collett was critical of Welhaven's work from a feminist standpoint, they did share the foundational concept of freedom. Anne-Lise Seip, *Demringstid. Johan Sebastian Welhaven og nasjonen* (Oslo: Aschehoug, 2007), 70–72; Ørjasæter, *Camilla*, 146–47. On the political aspects of romanticism, see also Anne K. Mellor, *Romanticism and Gender* (New York & London: Routledge, 1993); Beiser, *The Romantic Imperative.*

However, botany, belonging to the Enlightenment's natural history of classification, preceded biology as a model science.[30] The study of plants had an equally shifting aesthetic significance, as well as a long-lasting importance for communicating and bringing about women's emancipation. Amy M. King shows in her study *Bloom: The Botanical Vernacular in the English Novel*, that Carl Linnaeus' (1701–1778) plant taxonomy, his 'sexual system' or 'marriage of plants', became so popular and well-known that it could be used for novelistic ends. Botanical language became so pervasive that it could be used to convey complex social meanings. Linnaeus' works, mainly from the 1750s, were popularized from the 1770s onwards in numerous introductions aimed at a broad audience, including women and children.[31] King coins the concept the 'botanical vernacular' for a now forgotten representational system in science and in the novel of the late eighteenth and early nineteenth centuries.[32] The conflation of the natural and the social paved the way for novelistic use: Linnaeus' 'classificatory method terms the sexual reproduction of a flower *marriage*, a terminology that makes a horticultural fact a human fact, and by extension a human act (marriage) a horticultural, "natural" act (blooming)'.[33] In the eighteenth century, flowers became sexual organs, which is why bloom could represent sexual courtship.[34]

King traces what she calls the 'bloom narrative' in the nineteenth-century novel. The 'girl in bloom', that is the marriageable girl, is the centre figure of the narrative – in short, bloom was a way to talk about women's sexuality without offending the audience.[35] Of course, there was a long-standing tradition of flowers representing sexuality, including in the biblical *Song of Songs* and the medieval *Roman de la Rose*.[36] The pastoral representation of flowers, on the other hand, associated plants with sexual innocence – an even stronger literary tradition and still active in the nineteenth-century novel, which accounts for the use of the botanical vernacular as a successful veil for sexuality.[37] Linnaeus himself regarded the study of God's creation as an act of devotion – a reason why botany was considered fitting for women.[38] Whereas the professional botanists turned away from Linnaeus' taxonomy in the 1830s, the Linnean vernacular survived in the novel.[39] As such, the botanical vernacular and the bloom narrative

30 Amy M. King, *Bloom: The Botanical Vernacular in the English Novel* (Oxford & New York: Oxford University Press, 2003), 16.
31 King, *Bloom*, 17, 55–56.
32 King, *Bloom*, 6.
33 King, *Bloom*, 4.
34 King, *Bloom*, 3–4, 6, 11–47.
35 King, *Bloom*, 5.
36 King, *Bloom*, 6.
37 King, *Bloom*, 6, 63.
38 King, *Bloom*, 19, 53–54.
39 King, *Bloom*, 56–58.

also made their way into the Nordic emancipation novels. More importantly, melting together with the romantic idea of the organism and *Bildung*, the botanical vernacular gained a new significance as an argument for women's liberty.

Clinging vines, weed, and seeds of the Divine

The garden *topos* is ubiquitous in the Nordic emancipation novels of the 1850s. The most conspicuous use of the botanical vernacular as conceptual, argumentative metaphors is to be found in Bremer's *Hertha*. In a central passage, the main character Hertha discusses women's emancipation with Judge Carlson. The city Kungsköping has been burnt down to the ground, and the question is what part women will play in the new, rebuilt society. Hertha argues that there should be no limits to the issues that concern women, to which Judge Carlson objects by giving 'absurd descriptions of emancipated women'; the narrator summarises his account in stating that these descriptions 'have been too often produced, and are too well known, for there to be any necessity of our repeating them here'.[40] This is the cue for an organicist take on the botanical vernacular to take centre stage. Hertha replies:

> De karikaturer, ni nämner, ha uppkommit just af motsägelsen, såsom monstren bland blommorna uppkomma af brist på luft och ljus; de äro foster af en sträfvan, som ej funnit sitt rätta utlopp; de bevisa tillvaron af ett lif, en längtan, som förtjenade en bättre ledning. Gif den, genom rättvisa och kärlek; väck det högre medvetandet; ... gif dem frihet att bilda sig efter dessa förebilder, och skönheten skall skrämma bort karrikaturen. Missbildningarne, som ni talar om, skola försvinna som irrbloss vid solens uppgång.[41]
>
> The absurdities you mention have been produced from pure contradiction; in the same way that monsters among flowers are produced from deficiency of air and light; they are the offspring of an endeavour which has not found its proper vent. They prove the existence of a life, a longing which deserved a better guidance. Give this, by means of justice and love; awaken the higher consciousness; ... allow them liberty to form themselves according to this type, and beauty will then drive away the ridiculous. The educational abortions [literally: malformations] of which you speak will vanish as ignes-fatui at sunrise.[42]

40 Fredrika Bremer, *Hertha*, transl. Mary Howitt (London: Arthur Hall, Virtue & Co., 1856), 189. The original reads: 'Lagman Carlsson ... tecknade åtskilliga karrikatur-bilder af den emanciperade qvinnan, alltför ofta framställda och väl kända att vi skulle behöfva upprepa dem'. Fredrika Bremer, *Hertha, eller En själs historia. Teckning ur det verkliga lifvet*, eds. Åsa Arping and Gunnel Furuland (Stockholm: Svenska Vitterhetssamfundet, 2016), 133.

41 Bremer, *Hertha, eller En själs historia*, 133.

42 Bremer, *Hertha*, 189.

The simile deduces women's rights from an organicist logic; the flower imagery functions as a deliberate metaphor, intended to change Judge Carlson's – and the reader's – opinion. It is a conceptual metaphor, explaining women's emancipation in terms of the growth of plants, inviting the interlocutor to think of women's personal growth to be equally as natural as the growth of plants, and to consider the need for freedom of space as equally necessary for women as it is for flowers. In this case, the organicist imagery works as a theoretical underpinning of emancipation. Denise Gigante discusses the Romantic fascination with 'monstrous aberrations', and points out that the new evolution theory understood the monster differently from earlier periods; it 'defined a new mode of monstrosity'.[43] When the body was conceived of as preformed by God, aberrations made sense as 'material signs of God's judgement', but with the idea of evolution, when life was comprehended as equal to power, 'monstrosity came to represent life's relentless fecundity and "the monstrous" a mode of uncontainable vitality'.[44] In Bremer's use of the monster metaphor, God's plan is inherent in the natural growth, but the fecundity of life has been distorted by societal norms from developing according to that plan.

Mary Wollstonecraft also refuted the accusation that women are monsters in *A Vindication for the Rights of Woman*, but her *topos* for comparison was Roman emperors rather than the garden *topos*, and the monsters in her account are mostly men oppressing women.[45] She did indeed make ample use of flower imagery for women, but in a derogatory sense in line with the sexual connotations of the botanical vernacular. Women may, in Wollstonecraft's view, be 'like the flowers which are planted in too rich a soil, strength and usefulness are sacrificed to beauty', which she calls a 'barren blooming', and she scornfully notes that men class women 'with the smiling flowers that only adorn the land', clearly a reference to sexual licence.[46] The romantic, organicist framework had not yet reoriented the plant imagery to make it fit for theorizing the growth towards liberty. Wollstonecraft considered botany a suitable practice for women to sharpen reason and learn about sexuality, but flower imagery was obviously of no help to imagine liberation.[47]

However, nature did have a voice in Wollstonecraft's pamphlet, and on two occasions she refers to a tree as an analogue to the mind's need of time and experience to grow strong. Still, in those instances, Wollstonecraft could not trust

43 Gigante, *Life*, 48.

44 Gigante, *Life*, 6.

45 Mary Wollstonecraft, "A Vindication of the Rights of Woman" in *The Works of Mary Wollstonecraft: Vol. 5*, eds. Janet Todd and Marilyn Butler (London: William Pickering, 1989), 79–266, on monsters, see esp. p. 87, 105, 113–14, 177.

46 Wollstonecraft, "A Vindication of the Rights of Woman", 73, 122.

47 On botany in women's education, see King, *Bloom,* 50–58.

the reader to make the connection, but took pains to explain: 'There appears to be something analogous in the mind'.[48] The Tree of Knowledge, on the other hand, is referred to throughout the pamphlet, but in a purely rhetorical sense.[49] In contrast, Bremer's *Hertha*, as well as Collett's and Fibiger's emancipation novels, thematized and thoroughly investigated the biblical story of the Fall, including the Tree of Knowledge.[50] The tree in its organicist capacity, though, is mostly connected to the clinging vine in the emancipation novels of the 1850s.

Of course, the metaphor of women as clinging vines is a traditional, patriarchal trope. Still, as several researchers have noted, Fredrika Runeberg expanded on this very metaphor for feminist purposes on several occasions. The first instance is a short story entitled "Rankvexten" (The clinging vine), published in 1857 - that is, the year before the novel *Fru Catharina Boije och hennes döttrar.*[51] As Pia Forssell points out, Runeberg often used plant symbolism, and several of the stories in the subsequent collection of short stories have flower titles such as "Liljekonvaljen" (The lily of the valley), "Oleandern" (The oleander), and "Rosen" (The rose).[52] "Rankvexten" amounts to an allegory of the rights of women, where the trees clearly should be read as men while the clinging vines refer to women. The narrator is advised by a gardener, 'a man of the law', to plant a clinging vine seed on the shadowy side of the tree, since 'she is no good as an independent plant' anyway and needs proper binding; 'every sprout, that aspires to float through the air' should be cut.[53] However, the result 'surely cannot be the true

---

48 Wollstonecraft, "A Vindication of the Rights of Woman", 177, 183.

49 Wollstonecraft, "A Vindication of the Rights of Woman", for example 89, 160, 245.

50 For a thorough investigation of the Fall in Collett's, Bremer's, and Fibiger's novels, see Anna Bohlin, "Äppelträd och synd: Wergeland och de nordiska emancipationsromanerna" in *Ung må Wergeland ennå være: Sju artikler*, eds. Elin Stengrundet and Erik Bjerck Hagen (Bergen: Alvheim & Eide Akademisk Forlag, 2022), 11–33. See also Stefanie von Schnurbein, "Writing from the Margins: New voices in literature, social critique and the novel around 1850" in *Figurationen des Jüdischen: Spurensuchen in der skandinavischen Literatur.* Berliner Beiträge zur Skandinavistik, eds. Clemens Räthel and Stefanie von Schnurbein (Berlin: Nordeuropa-Institut der Humboldt-Universität zu Berlin, 2020), 235–58, discussion of the Fall on p. 40.

51 The short story was published once more in her collection of stories *Teckningar och drömmar* (1861, Sketches and dreams). Forssell, "Fredrika Runeberg mellan familjeideologi och emancipation", 109–10; Forssell, "Sigrid Liljeholm och kvinnorollens gränser," 70–71; Mazzarella, *Fredrika Charlotta född Tengström.*

52 Pia Forssell explores different types of trees as emblems for different social classes and 'vegetative symbolism' in the portrayal of the eponymous heroine in Runeberg's second novel *Sigrid Liljeholm* (1862). Pia Forssell, "Sigrid Liljeholm och kvinnorollens gränser", *Historiska och litteraturhistoriska studier* 69 (1994): 21–83, see esp. p. 52, 70–71.

53 The Swedish original reads: 'en lagens man'; 'icke duger hon till självständig vext'; 'skär bort alla skott, som vilja sväfva i luften'. -a -g [Fredrika Runeberg], "Rankvexten" in *Teckningar och drömmar* (Helsingfors: Theodor Sederholms förlag, 1861), 74–76, quotation on p. 74. There is to my knowledge no English translation of this short-story, and the translations are, therefore, my own.

nature of your being', the narrator thinks, and plants a second seed by another tree 'with equal share of God's sun and air and day', and allows it to grow freely.[54] As in Bremer's *Hertha*, trust in God's creation is the ultimate argument in this case:

> Behöfver Gud hjelp af menniskolagens tvång, för att få sin skapelse fulländad; .... Jag såg ju, huru i Guds fria sköna verld allt artade sig väl utan bojor och band, och jag trodde på min ranka.[55]

> Does God need help from the constraint of human law to perfect his creation; .... Surely I could see how everything in God's free beautiful world developed well without shackles and bonds, and I believed in my clinging vine.

The outcome of this free upbringing is the 'harmonious' intertwinement of tree and clinging vine, from which the tree grows 'ever more grand' and the clinging vine 'softer and richer'.[56] To grow softer might not seem very encouraging to a modern-day feminist, but it was a key point in Runeberg's romantic understanding of femininity.[57]

The clinging vine interestingly resurfaces in a pivotal scene in Runeberg's emancipation novel from 1858, *Fru Catharina Boije och hennes döttrar*, which features two sisters. Margaretha and Cecilia are portrayed as opposites in several ways; Cecilia is the romantic character of the two. Their destinies are also reversed. At the end of the novel, Margaretha is allowed to live happily ever after in Finland with her low-born husband, whereas Cecilia dies from horror on the morning of her wedding to a despicably immoral Swedish nobleman, scornful of women as well as of everything Finnish.[58] On the evening prior to her wedding, seconds before the shock of fear that will lead to her death, Cecilia reflects on her impossible situation. On the one hand, she is bound by her duty to love her future

54 The Swedish original reads: 'så var visst icke ditt väsendes rätta art'; 'dela lika af Guds sol och luft och dag'. Runeberg, "Rankvexten", 75.

55 Runeberg, "Rankvexten", 76.

56 The Swedish original reads: 'harmoniskt'; 'Allt större och präktigare vexte mitt träd, allt mjukare och rikare min ranka'. Runeberg, "Rankvexten," 76.

57 Pia Forssell stresses that Runeberg's first novel and her collection of stories were well received by the press and suggests that the reason was that they were not in fact more radical in terms of women's education than the leading critics' (and Runeberg's friends) Zacharias Topelius and J.V. Snellman views on women's emancipation. Forssell, "Fredrika Runeberg mellan familjeideologi och emancipation," 110.

58 This romance was indeed part of Finnish nation building. On nation building in *Fru Catharina Boije och hennes döttrar*, see Mari Hatavara, "History, the Historical Novel and Nation. The First Finnish Historical Novels as National Narrative," *Neophilologus* 86 (2002): 1–15; Grönstrand, "Historical Fiction and the Dynamics of Romance"; Kristina Malmio, "Affective Bodies on the Move: Space, Emotions and Loss in Fredrika Runeberg's Historical Novel Lady Catharina and her Daughters" in *Nineteenth-Century Nationalisms and Emotions in the Nordic Region: The Production of Loss*, eds. Anna Bohlin, Tiina Kinnunen, and Heidi Grönstrand (Leiden & Boston: Brill, 2021), 192–218.

husband, but on the other hand, knowing his true nature, she cannot love him. The deadly outcome of this paradox of feelings is explained with organicist imagery – once again a conceptual metaphor suggesting a theorization. She compares herself to a clinging vine:

> Jag såg en gång en rankvext, den hade slingrat sig om en ung telning, ett vackert, rakt träd. Jag gick så gerna och såg på det paret. Men rankan dog, och så var det slut. År hade sedan förgått, och jag såg samma träd maskstunget, förvridet och murknadt i kärnan; då var jag glad, att rankan dog medan trädet stod i sin fägring. Den var ju med hvarje tråd fästad vid trädet och skulle ändå haft sitt lif endast med det murkna och förvridna.[59]

> I once saw a clinging vine, trailed around a young sapling, a beautiful, straight tree. It pleased me to watch that pair. But the clinging vine died, and that was the end. Years went by, and I saw that same tree worm-eaten, twisted, and rotted to the heart; then I was glad, that the clinging vine died while the tree was blooming. It was bound up to the tree with every fibre and would anyhow have had its life solely with the rotted and twisted.

Cecilia goes on to explicitly identify herself with the clinging vine in saying that 'my tree has begun to rot in its heart'.[60] The organicist mini-allegory explains why her death is imminent; being inextricably tied to the immoral Swedish man, she is practically already dead. Thus, the metaphor has an argumentative function, intended to convince the reader of the urgent need for women's emancipation.

The clinging vine also depicts the situation of women in Danish Mathilde Fibiger's emancipation novel *Clara Raphael*, but in a positive and slightly different conceptual metaphor – the tree in this case explicitly refers to God. In the third letter, Clara questions men's right to oppress women, and places some of the blame on women for being tempted to please others, which results in dependence. The answer is of course to resist temptation and stay close to God, which in the letter's closing proclamation is clarified by an organicist analogy: 'Som Slyngplanten, der støtter sig til den mægtige Eeg, skulde vi støtte os til Gud, og drage Liv og Næring af den evige Viisdoms Kilde' (like the clinging vine, trailing around the powerful oak, we should lean on God, and draw life and nourishment from the eternal source of wisdom).[61] God himself is a tree providing sustenance in several respects, according to this deliberate and argumentative metaphor.

---

59 -a -g [Fredrika Runeberg], *Fru Catharina och hennes döttrar. En berättelse från stora ofredens tid* (Helsingfors: Finska Litteratur-sällskapets tryckeri, 1858), 223. There is to my knowledge no English translation of Runeberg's novel, and the translations are therefore my own.

60 The Swedish original reads: 'mitt träd har tagit röta i kärnan'. Runeberg, *Fru Catharina*, 223.

61 Mathilde Fibiger, *Clara Raphael. Tolv Breve* (Copenhagen: Reitzel, 1851), 26. There is to my knowledge no English translation of Fibiger's novel, and the translations are therefore my own.

God is also the force that brings 'every seed in my soul to grow and develop', Clara claims in another organicist metaphor, which is further elaborated on in a key passage that legitimizes women's emancipation:

> Gud skabte Mennesket i sit Billede. .... Saaledes ligger Spiren til det guddommelige Liv i os, begravet i vor Sjæl. Lad os luge det Ukrud af, som er opvoxet derover, plante Spiren hen i Oplysningens Solskin, og den vil snart udfolde sig til den yndigste Blomst.[62]

> God created Man in his own image. ... . Therefore the germ to divine life is within us, buried in our soul. Let us weed out what has grown over it, plant the germ in the sunshine of enlightenment, and it will soon develop into the loveliest of flowers.

The sexual connotation of the botanical vernacular is thoroughly rooted out in Fibiger's account in favour of the romantic double exposition of the soul and the landscape in relation to God. The argument for women's liberation rests securely on the conflation of the double meaning of *Bildung*, on the one hand referring to Man as the image of God, and on the other hand to the romantic conception of inner growth. To be sure, the word of God as seed has a biblical origin, especially in the parable of the sower and the parable of the weeds (Mark 4:1–20; Matthew 13:1–30), but Fibiger transforms the biblical imagery into an organicist version where the goal is the growth of a lovely flower as a result of access to sunshine. In Bremer's novel, the 'monsters among the flowers' had not had the opportunity to develop according to God's plan, and the weeds covering the seeds of Divine life in Fibiger's argumentative metaphor represent society's hindering of women's emancipation. However, the political use of the botanical vernacular takes on a more complex set of meanings in Collett's emancipation novel.

Competing interpretations of flowers in *The District Governor's Daughters*

Collett makes ample use of the flower imagery, and even explores the *topos* of the garden with conflicting meanings. The bloom narrative, as King defines it, recalling sexuality and desire, is activated in core moments of the plot, suggesting deliberate metaphors with an argumentative function. The head character Sophie 'bloomed like a rose' when in love with the romantic hero Cold, whereas her eldest sister Maria married a Pietist priest who denied her every pleasure and, subsequently, she has no children and dies from boredom: 'She withered like a plant in a botanist's case'.[63] Happiness is not to be trusted in this

62 The original of the first quotation reads: 'Guds vidunderlige Kraft ... bringer hvert Frø i min Sjæl til at spire og udvikle sig'. Fibiger, *Clara Raphael*, 42, 54–55.

63 Camilla Collett, *The District Governor's Daughters*, English translation by Kirsten Seaver

novel, and shortly after Sophie's happy love episode, she overhears Cold denying his love for her. The tragedy of this love story is that the denial is a lie, but because of societal norms, that misunderstanding will not be resolved until it is too late.

Still, the bloom narrative permeates the text even after the turning point in the romantic love story. On the morning after the fatal misunderstanding, Sophie is reflecting on her misfortune in studying a flower. She is walking in the garden, at times stopping

> grublende foran en Blomst, som om hun vilde studere hver Aare i dens Blade. Men det var kun sin Ulykke hun studerede paa, det var alle de fine Traade, hvoraf denne havde udspundet sig, hun bestræbte sig for at samle.[64]

> in order to brood in front of a flower, as if she wished to study each vein in its petals. But it was only her unhappiness she was brooding over. She was trying hard to gather all the fine threads of which it was spun.[65]

The narrator suggests that Sophie is a flower herself and that the threads of her destiny are legible in the veins of the flower petals. The bloom narrative is strengthened when she a moment later blames herself for having spoken of her love before Cold: 'She had said the word *before he did* – not consciously and as a result of her own will, but as naturally as a flower unfolding when its time has come'.[66] In the third, and partly rewritten edition of 1879, Collett reinforced the organicist imagery: 'as easily as a fruit drops from the branch by its own weight…'[67]

The political use of the bloom narrative in Collett's novel ventures in two directions: first, as a criticism of patriarchal norms by invoking the sexual connotations of the botanical vernacular, and second, as a depiction of the core value of emancipation. Cold turns out to be a botanist, well-versed in Linnean taxonomy: 'He recognized each little family of flowers'.[68] He also proves to be well

(London: Norvik Press, 2017), 142, 271. The original reads: 'blomstrede som en Rose'; 'Hun visnede, hun, som Planten i Botaniserkassen'. Camilla Collett, *Amtmandens Døttre I–II* (Christiania: Johan Dahl, 1854–1855), I, 200; II, 225.

64 Collett, *Amtmandens Døttre,* II, 97.

65 Collett, *The District Governor's Daughters*, 204.

66 Collett, *The District Governor's Daughters*, 205. The original reads: 'Hun havde udtalt Ordet *før ham*, ikke bevidst og villiestærk, men saa naturligt som Blomsterkalken, der aabner sig i rette Tid…' Collett, *Amtmandens Døttre,* II, 98–99.

67 Collett, *The District Governor's Daughters*, 205. The original reads: 'som Frugten, der løsnes fra Grenen ved sin egen Tyngde…' Camilla Collett, *Amtmandens Døtre* (Kristiania: Alb. Cammermeyers Forlag, 1879), 113.

68 The narrator goes on to specify a number of flowers on his path through the garden and across the meadows. Collett, *The District Governor's Daughters*, 299. The original reads: 'Hver Busk hilsede ham som en gammel Ven, han kjendte hver særskilt lille Blomsterfamilie igjen'. Collett, *Amtmandens Døttre*, II, 280.

informed of the sexual connotations, when he lies to his friend that he has seduced Sophie for fun: 'It is but another flower to be braided into my triumphal wreath'.[69] And to Sophie, in the final scene when the misunderstanding is cleared, he refers to the same interpretation of flowers when he asks her: 'Have I not shielded my fragile flower?'[70] Collett chides the patriarchal conceptual metaphor of the botanical vernacular to refer to the sexual use of women, but the very same connotations allow her to engage the flower metaphors in defining women's emancipation.

In fact, Collett's most succinct formulation of women's emancipation is entirely couched in the botanical vernacular. Love is the centre of Collett's emancipatory project, connecting women's contribution to society to a romantic understanding of femininity.[71] The definition of emancipation is proclaimed by Margrethe, Cold's mature friend, who dies and leaves behind a diary, documenting the sufferings of emancipated women. Love is indeed the source of women's emancipation, Margrethe states, but only on one condition:

> Men saa maae denne Kjærlighed først emanciperes, det er: reddes fra Barbarie og Trældom. Beskyt da, o Menneskehed! denne vort Livs første Blomst, thi det er af den al Velsignelse siden skal modnes. Agt paa dens Væxt og Frugt.... Forstyr ikke letsindig dens fine Hjerteblade i den stupide Troe, at de grove Blade siden ere gode nok... Nei, de ere ikke gode nok.[72]

> this love must first be liberated, i.e. freed from barbarism and slavery. Oh humanity, protect this first flower of our lives, because all subsequent blessings must come from it. Take heed of its growth and fruits.... Do not frivolously disturb its fragile central leaf [literally 'heart leaves'] in the stupid belief that the coarse leaves succeeding it are good enough.... No, they are not good enough.[73]

The liberated love is in Collett's account a 'first flower', a political capacity inherent in the organism, as Schiller would have it.[74] In line with the romantic, organicist logic, recognizable from the other Nordic emancipation novels of the 1850s, love will grow and bear fruits.

The opposite of the politically potent love, the 'coarse leaves' in the quotation above, is further exemplified by Cold's earlier inclinations. In Margrethe's view: 'It was that *artificial* hothouse sentiment, the green fruit of *coincidence*; it was the

69 Collett, *The District Governor's Daughters*, 200. The original reads: 'Det er blot en ny Blomst, jeg fletter ind i mine Seiervindingers Krands'. Collett, *Amtmandens Døttre*, I, 89.

70 Collett, *The District Governor's Daughters*, 304. The original reads: 'Har jeg ikke skaanet min fine Blomst?' Collett, *Amtmandens Døttre*, II, 288.

71 See f.ex. Steinfeld, *Camilla Collett: Ungdom og ekteskap*, 440–41; Ørjasæter, "Camilla Colletts kristne feminisme"; Ørjasæter, *Camilla: Norges første feminist.*

72 Collett, *Amtmandens Døttre*, I, 160.

73 Collett, *The District Governor's Daughters*, 122.

74 Gigante, *Life*, 25.

feeble reflection of masculine desire, which arises from an interplay between flattered vanity, commonsensical calculation, and an inherited habit of submission'.[75] King points out that the first artificial flower in 1717, a human-designed hybrid between a carnation and a sweet william, was referred to as 'monstrous' because they could not reproduce.[76] Fertility, in both a literal and a figurative sense, is indeed a core issue in Collett's concept of emancipated love, unveiled by the botanical vernacular. However, heart leaves, fruits, and coarse leaves would, in Collett's later essays, be replaced by animals.

Transition from plants to animals in Collett's essays

The opening quotation on the spread of emancipation as pollination deserves to be quoted in full. The introduction to Collett's essay "Om Kvinden og hendes Stilling" (On the woman and her position) from 1872, ends with the following vision of the future:

> En Dag vil komme, da Sagen forløser sig selv. Bevidstheden om dens Ret vil da have gjennemtrængt hele Samfundsatmosfæren. Vi indaande den med Luften, den vil gaa som Blomsterstøvet med Vinden, usynlig, ufattelig, og med uimodstaaelig Magt vil den gribe Alle, baade Underkuerne og de Forkuede.
>
> A day will come, when the cause will deliver itself. The awareness of its right will by then have penetrated the atmosphere of the entire society. We will breathe it in with the air, it will disseminate like pollen carried by the wind, invisible, incomprehensible, and with irresistible power, it will capture everyone, the oppressors and the oppressed alike.[77]

Collett predicts that women's emancipation will act with 'irresistible power', a law of nature, that cannot be contradicted. In future, liberty will become as natural and as necessary to society as air, to the point that women's rights will be achieved without any active interference; 'the cause will deliver itself'. Women's rights will be part of nature, according to Collett's divination – an idea completely foreign to Wollstonecraft's line of thought. In the very last sentence of the introduction, Collett goes on to enforce the organicist imagery in connection to progress: 'these fruitful seeds will be shaken down in thousands and we will be pulled decades closer to the fulfilment'.[78] The use of the bloom narrative in arguments

75 Collett, *The District Governor's Daughters*, 119. The original reads: 'Det var den *uægte*, Drivhuusfølelsen, *Tilfældighedens* umodne Frugt, det var denne matte Reflex af Mandens Begjær, der opstaaer af et Sammenspil af smigret Forfængelighed, fornuftig Beregning og en nedarvet Underkastelsesvane'. Collett, *Amtmandens Døttre*, I, 154–55, Collett's italics.

76 King, *Bloom*, 71.

77 Collett, "Om Kvinden og hendes Stilling", 60, my translation.

78 Collett, "Om Kvinden og hendes Stilling", 60, my translation. The original reads: '[der] rystes … Tusinder af disse frugtbringende Frø ned og [vi] drages … Aartier nærmere Opfyldelsen'.

for women's emancipation has shifted from Wollstonecraft's derogatory sense of immoral, sexual licence, over the mid-nineteenth-century theoretical underpinning to claims on personal *Bildung*, to a stress on an organic understanding of society. Political progress inherent to matter was no longer restricted to the individual body but encompassed society as a whole; progress was no longer necessarily a result of God's plan, but could certainly be explained by evolutionary biology. The notion of women's liberty permeating the society as pollination suggests that society is an organism.

As Tone Selboe notes, Collett herself never used the term 'essay' about the collections she published in 1868–1885, several of them under the title *Sidste Blade. Erindringer og Bekjendelser* (Last papers: memories and confessions).[79] They include different kinds of texts, usually first published in periodicals: travel letters (mostly from European cities such as Berlin, Paris, Rome) and literary criticism, letters to public persons, short aphoristic texts as well as long essays. Women's emancipation is a recurrent theme throughout these texts, and "Kvinden i Literaturen" (The woman in literature) in *Fra de stummes Lejr* (From the camp of the speechless) from 1877 is perhaps the first example of feminist literary criticism in Norwegian literary history.[80] Collett chides the patriarchal society in general and Norwegian society in particular, often with an irony verging on sarcasm.

Selboe observes that Collett assumes an '*avant-garde position*' in her essays, appearing as a champion of the future, 'the soldier on the front line'.[81] The entire authorship, Selboe writes, 'is driven by a desire for change and improvement on behalf of the future generations'.[82] That driving force is incorporated into an idea of progress that takes on connotations of evolutionary biology. Collett constantly made sense of women's emancipation in terms of progress, and she put her faith in the future. As a Norwegian female writer, Collett perceived herself as someone who had 'foregrebet Tiden' (anticipated time itself), she was 50 years ahead of time to be precise, according to the preface to her first collection of essays from 1868.[83] The militaristic imagery that Selboe draws attention to is complemented by the *topos* of a legal case. Already in her very first published article, "Strikketøisbetragtninger" (Knitting reflections) from 1843, she writes about the 'Spindesidens Dom over Sværdsiden' (The spinning side's judgment on the

79 Tone Selboe, *Camilla Collett: Engasjerte essays* (Oslo: Aschehoug, 2013), 16.

80 Selboe, *Engasjerte essays*, 27.

81 Selboe, *Engasjerte essays*, 19, my translation.

82 Selboe, *Engasjerte essays*, 22, my translation.

83 Camilla Collett, "Brev til Fru Amalie Munch" in *Sidste Blade. Erindringer og Bekjendelser* (Copenhagen: Gyldendalske Boghandel, 1868), 1–12.

spear side).[84] The juridical imagery is present throughout her published essays; in the introduction to the aforementioned "Kvinden i Literaturen", she states the legal case between the two parties of company Man: Eve vs Adam 'for tusindaarige Mishandlinger og Misbrug af Magten' (for thousands of years of maltreatment and abuse of power).[85] However, the organicist imagery serves as a conceptual metaphor for the progress of women's rights and shows an increasing presence of animals.

In an essay dated 1873, animals enter the organicist imagery as a model for human behaviour. In Wollstonecraft's *A Vindication of the Rights of Woman*, animal life is perhaps not an opposite of desirable human behaviour, but it is certainly perceived as a stage prior to virtue and reason when she, for instance, scolds women who content themselves with being dependent on a husband for being 'scarcely raised by her employments above the animal kingdom'.[86] A hundred years later, in Collett's essay "Fra et mindre hjemligt Standpunkt" (From a less homelike standpoint) from 1873, animal virtues are portrayed as superior to humans. Collett ridicules the idea that physical strength is evidence of a spiritual strength that legitimizes the right to rule. She gives a number of examples from the animal kingdom of 'households and small states of living creatures … that honour the opposite principle. Here strength did not earn *prerogatives*; but called for *obligations*'.[87] One of the examples is 'a small state, where the only female was raised to absolute ruler, while all the males were workers!'[88] Whereas the bee colony in this instance is elevated to a matriarchal model, the bees will in the next instance serve as representatives of patriarchal exploitation, when Collett once more activates the bloom narrative. She assures the reader that she is acquainted with many noble men, but that many men 'equally naturally, you could almost say innocently, occupy their women's faculty of will and right to self-determination, just like bees suck out the nearest flower-cup'.[89] The romantic

84 Camilla Collett, "Strikketøisbetragtninger" [1843] in *Sidste Blade: Fjerde og femte Række* (Christiania: P.T. Mallings Boghandel, 1873), 41–53, quotation on p. 44.

85 Camilla Collett, "Kvinden i Literaturen" in *Fra de stummes Lejr* (Christiania: P. T. Mallings boghandel, 1877), 7.

86 Wollstonecraft, "A Vindication of the Rights of Woman," 101.

87 The original reads: 'af levende Væseners Husholdninger og Smaastater … set det modsatte Princip hyldet. Her tilvandt Styrken sig ikke *Prærogativer*; men den paalagde *Forpligtelser*'. Camilla Collett, "Fra et et mindre hjemligt standpunkt" in *Samlede Verker II* (Kristiania & København: Gyldendal Boghandel Nordisk Forlag, 1913), 346–53, quotation on p. 350, my translation.

88 The original reads: 'en liden Stat, hvori det eneste Femininum, der fandtes, var ophøiet til Eneherskerinde, medens alle Maskulinerne var Arbeidere!' Collett, "Fra et et mindre hjemligt standpunkt", 350.

89 The original reads: 'ligesaa naturlig, man kan næsten sige uskyldig, udbytter sine Kvinders Viljesformue og Selvbestemmelseret, som Bien udsuger den nærmeste Blomsterklase'. Collett, "Fra et mindre hjemligt standpunkt". 351.

organicist imagery has been displaced by imagery inviting Darwinist thought. Animals may not always be ethically superior to humans, but in contrast to Wollstonecraft's statement, they may be compared on an equal footing. Ellen Key quoted extensively and approvingly from this passage of Collett's essay in her first published article, an overview of Collett's authorship.[90] Key's comprehensive article on Collett highlighted Collett's organicist imagery that made thinking about women's liberty in Darwinist terms possible.

At the turn of the twentieth century, animals would be a frequent point of reference as models and comparisons in feminist theory. Most feminist theorists based their claims about women's emancipation on various versions of Darwinism, and women's situation in contemporary society was explained by way of a natural history of evolutionary biology. For example, the influential American feminist Charlotte Perkins Gilman (1860–1935) analysed women's position as a result of the imbalance between 'self-preservation' and 'race-preservation', and the equally famous South African women's rights activist Olive Schreiner (1855–1920) warned that women's current position would lead to the degeneration of the human race, whereas Ellen Key understood society as an organism built of sexed 'cells'.[91] These theorists subscribed – to a larger or lesser extent – to the statement that women's most important task in promoting emancipation would be to choose the right fathers for their children; the future was to be found in bodies, or in the inheritance to be precise.[92] Inhaling women's rights with the atmosphere as pollen, as Collett suggested, would simply no longer do the trick; emancipation required pollination in a sexual, more literal sense.

Emancipation itself takes on a body on several occasions in Collett's essays. Earlier in the introduction to "Om Kvinden og hendes Stilling", she urges emancipation to acquire arms, wings, eyes, and voice in order to move public opinion.[93] In an essay written in July 1870, emancipation becomes a child, 'Afføding af den moderne Civilisation' (an offspring of modern civilisation), presented by 'Time', and Time itself is in distress in "Kvinden i Literaturen" and calls for women to exercise their powers to set progress right.[94] The personification of Time is obviously a classic trope, but when it is used to visualize progress, the

90 Key, "Camille Collet [sic] och hennes författareverksamhet," 262–77. See also Bohlin, "Camilla Collett – den felande länken i svensk litteraturhistoria".

91 Charlotte Perkins Gilman, *Women and Economics: A Study of the Economic Relation Between Men and Women as a Factor in Social Evolution* (Boston: Small, Meynard & Co, 1898); Olive Schreiner, *Woman and Labour* (London: T. Fisher Unwin, 1911); Ellen Key, *Lifslinjer I: Kärleken och äktenskapet* (Stockholm: Bonnier (1903).

92 See for example Bohlin, *Röstens anatomi*, 79–85, 146–53, 380–90.

93 Collett, "Om Kvinden og hendes Stilling," 56.

94 Camilla Collett, "Fra et hjemligt Standpunkt" in *Sidste Blade: Fjerde og femte Række* (Christiania: P.T. Mallings Boghandel, 1873), 163–74, quotation on p. 168; Collett, "Kvinden i Literaturen," 6.

corporeality of the personification comes to the fore. In these cases, the personifications of Time and Emancipation work as deliberate metaphors to convince the reader of the necessity of women's rights, and they suggest that the future is dependent on bodies.

In "Om Kvinden og hendes Stilling", Collett compares the situation of women to that of ladybirds who apparently eat each other for lack of proper nourishment – not a pleasant habit, but an effective way to show nature's response to bad conditions. 'Da vor Aand savne den naturlige, kraftige Føde' (since our spirit lacks the natural, nutritious food), Collett writes, 'kaster den sig paa en indbyrdes, paa Personalkritiken og frister Livet ved den' (it turns on each other with personal criticism, risking life); she longs for the day when the starving woman's spirit is satisfied.[95] That parable could never have occurred in any of the emancipation novels twenty years earlier; it is far too coarse and, above all, treats a despicable animal behaviour as relevant to understanding human society. The ladybirds are an indication of the shift of conceptual metaphors.

The following essay is entitled "Dyreskikkelser" (Animal figures) which, of course, recalls the fable, a genre with a long literary history from Aesop to Hans Christian Andersen's "The Ugly Duckling". However, the animals in Collett's account are, in contrast to the traditional fable, not projections of human society. She even hopes that they do not have a conscious mind considering how badly they are treated by humans and, anyway, their fine instincts put human feelings to shame. Admittedly, women's rights are not the issue here, but Collett problematizes on a somewhat joking note the distinction between the animal and the human. Contrary to Wollstonecraft, Collett gives the animal instincts moral precedence over human society. Her observations on the animals' superior behaviour includes a cuckoo boy, who – as is the cuckoo's way – is hatched in a small bird's nest and still not abandoned by 'den kjerlige Pleiemoder' (the loving foster mother), and an old gander, who sticks to his old goose wife, taking no notice of the attractive young geese.[96] Still, the end of the essay taps into the fable. The narrator tells us that birds are able to speak human languages on certain feast days, and the animals use this opportunity to speak back. It turns out that the cuckoo story has been treated by a bird playwright of tragedies who lets the cuckoo eat up the foster mother to create a more dramatic story – the violent death is an instance of literary imagination. Collett poses the question of whether the violence should be considered animal or human. The generic characteristics of the fable is thus used to question the distinction between humans and animals instead of upholding it. Her treatment of animals on the same level as humans

95 Collett, "Om Kvinden og hendes Stilling", 69–70.

96 Camilla Collett, "Dyreskikkelser" in *Sidste Blade. Erindringer og Bekjendelser. Anden og tredie Række* (Christiania: P. L. Malling, 1872), 119–23, quotation on p. 120.

substantiates the transformation of the deliberate metaphors in her arguments for women's liberation. It has become closer at hand to portray human societies through animals than through plants.

Concluding remarks

We need to pay more attention to the imagery when examining nineteenth-century literature leading up to the women's movement and twentieth-century feminist theory. At pivotal moments in the Nordic emancipation novels of the 1850s, organicist imagery is used as deliberate metaphors with an argumentative function to legitimize, explain, and make sense of women's emancipation. The growth of plants are used to convince the reader of the necessity of freedom for women to develop the seeds in their souls according to God's purpose, depicting societal conditions as weeds to be cleared away. The patriarchal metaphor of women as clinging vines is converted into a feminist use by turning the attention to the disastrous consequences of the rotting tree or featuring God as the only tree to provide nourishment. In Collett's *The District Governor's Daughters*, the 'botanical vernacular' is used both for criticism of patriarchal norms for sexuality and for conveying politically potent love as the core value of women's emancipation. The organicist metaphors thus specify how Collett, Fibiger, Bremer, and Runeberg conceived of women's rights within a romantic understanding of *Bildung* in connection to a Christian notion of evolution; the imagery suggests a theoretical conception of emancipation. However, in Collett's essays from the 1870s, the organicist imagery is displaced from flowers to animals; the figures of emancipation increasingly suggest a perception of women's rights as a law of nature. In Wollstonecraft's pamphlet from 1792, animals represented a stage prior to virtue and reason – her tools for promoting women's rights – whereas Collett's essays, on the contrary, suggest that women's emancipation will benefit from comparisons with the animal world. Feminist ideas of progress were in the process of being transformed from *Bildung* to Darwinist evolutionary biology.

Alda Björk Valdimarsdóttir
(University of Iceland)

"… the really accomplished young woman, which she wanted to be thought herself;" Jane Austen, the chick lit genre, self-help culture, and 18th-century conduct books

Abstract
This article will focus on the impact the novelist Jane Austen has had on the modern chick lit genre more than two hundred years after her death and further raise the question of whether the characteristics of the genre can provide insights into the role of self-improvement in Austen's work, taking *Pride and Prejudice* and *Emma* as an example, with a special emphasis on her flawed heroines. Austen's heroines generally do not fit the perfect image of femininity depicted in the conduct books that were popular in the 18th and 19th centuries, just as the modern chick lit heroines do not represent the ideas of desirable femininity. Austen engages purposeful dialogue with contemporary conduct books in her novels, just like modern chick lit authors converse with glossy magazines. In addition, many heroines are devoted readers of various self-help books. It is argued that both Austen's novels and the chick lit genre draw out the tension between private and public spheres, the stories predicting limited egress for their female heroines since the public sphere is a reality they have minimal access to. Because of that, the heroines ward off boredom through their fantastic tales or find an outlet through lies, spin-offs, and laughter to survive in a patriarchal society.

Keywords
Jane Austen, chick lit, conduct books, Elízabeth Bennet, Emma Woodhouse, Becky Bloomwood.

This article will focus on the impact the novelist Jane Austen has had on the modern chick lit genre more than two hundred years after her death and further raise the question of whether the characteristics of the genre can provide insights into the role of self-improvement in Austen's work, taking *Pride and Prejudice* and *Emma* as an example.

Austen's emphasis on comical female characters that are flawed is a central theme of the chick lit novel and drives the plot forward, as is suggested in a letter to her niece Fanny Knight: "Pictures of perfection as you know make me sick & wicked." About graceful and decent Anne Elliot, Austen famously said in the same letter, "You may *perhaps* like the Heroine, as she is almost too good for me".[1] This draws attention to the fact that the perfect and reliable heroine of *Persuasion* was an unusual female protagonist for the novelist since she is without the traits that are associated with her more comical and flawed sister characters.

Chick lit novels give the effect of realism by showing defective heroines, and this results in readers perhaps finding identification with them relatively easily. As Ferriss and Young have pointed out, the heroine deploys self-deprecating humour; she can be rude, shallow, overly compulsive, neurotic, insecure, bold, ambitious, or witty,[2] but "we love her anyway" (or maybe because of it). This opposition to perfection encourages an ironic reading of chick lit novels, their heroines follow contemporary norms, but their pursuits are also marked by desperation because the yearning for a new identity and a better life is both demanding and draining. The novels mockingly undermine their character's interest in entertainment, consumerism, and advertisement culture. Stephanie Harzewski captures the idea well when she describes Helen Fielding's *Bridget Jones's Diary* (1996) as "the ironic novel of development."[3]

How would the idea of reading chick lit in terms of the ironic bildungsroman relate to contemporary interests in Jane Austen's work and her authorial image, especially the idea of self-empowerment and personal growth? Chick lit is similar to many self-help books and conduct manuals in its focus on self-improvement and manners, and in this light, it is interesting to think of the many personal empowerment books that have been produced under the guise of Austen in recent years, works such as Henderson's *Jane Austen's Guide to Dating* and Hannon's *Dear Jane Austen: A Heroine's Guide to Life and Love.*[4] Here, Austen's novels are rewritten in the form of self-help guides using as exemplary models various illustrative scenes from the author's works to improve the reader's social and love life.

This interest in Austen as an authority on social refinement is often interwoven with contemporary conservative ideas about womanhood in the Regency period as can be seen in various contemporary self-help books, such as *The Jane Austen Guide to Life:Thoughtful Lessons for the Modern Woman* by Lori Smith,[5]

1 See Jane Austen (March 23–25th 1817), "To Fanny Knight", *Jane Austen's Letters*, ed. Deirdre Le Faye, (Oxford and New York: Oxford University Press, 1995), 335.

2 Suzanne Ferriss and Mallory Young, "Introduction", *Chick Lit. The New Woman's Fiction*, ed. Suzanne Ferriss and Mallory Young (New York and London: Routledge, 2006), 4.

3 Stephanie Harzewski, *Chick Lit and Postfeminism*, (Charlottesville and London: University of Virginia Press, 2011), 61.

4 Patrice Hannon, *Dear Jane Austen: A Heroine's Guide to Life and Love*, (New York, A Plume Book, 2005) and Lauren Henderson, *Jane Austen's Guide to Dating*, (New York, Hyperion, 2005).

5 Lori Smith, *The Jane Austen Guide to Life: Thoughtful Lessons for the Modern Woman*, (Guilford, CT, Skirt!, 2012).

where Austen's texts become a conduct guide for bewildered women in present-day society.[6] Countless modern novels based on the authorial image of Austen have also been written from this reactionary viewpoint, where she acts as an instructor, a romance counsellor, and a matchmaker to the main protagonists who seem to discover themselves while searching for love under the guidance of Austen.[7]

As the female protagonists of chick lit are frequently presented as somewhat bewildered individuals who desire improvement, self-help culture is an integral part of the genre. Their absolute failure to live up to social norms and conventions generally leaves them desperate, indicating similarities between the sister genres chick lit and self-help books, which is also revealed through the sheer volume of works attempting to bridge the gap between the two,[8] e. g. when the heroines of chick lit novels make use of self-help culture in the hope of bettering themselves and their lives.[9]

Women's rabid appetite: Austen and chick lit as a genre

Austen's impact on chick lit fiction can be seen from the very start, as Fielding's *Bridget Jones's Diary* is a modern reimagining of *Pride and Prejudice* and is regarded as a cornerstone within the genre.[10] Darcy, the main male character in

---

6 Other self-help books working from this premise are Henrietta Webb, *Jane Austen's Guide to Good Manners: Compliments, Charades & Horrible Blunders* (London, Bloomsbury Publishing, 2006), Rebecca Smith, *Jane Austen's Guide to Modern Life's Dilemmas* (Lewes, East Sussex, Ivy Press, 2012), Margaret C. Sullivan, *The Jane Austen Handbook: Proper Life Skills from Regency England* (Philadelphia, PA, Quirk Books, 2007), and Sinead Murphy, *The Jane Austen Rules: A Classic Guide to Modern Love* (London, Melville House, 2014).

7 See for example *Austenland* by Shannon Hale, (New York, NY, Bloomsbury, 2007) and the film adaptation from 2013 starring Keri Russell). See also novels by Beth Pattillo *Mr. Darcy Broke My Heart* (New York, Guideposts, 2010) and *Jane Austen Ruined My Life* (New York, Guideposts, 2009). Other stories portray characters who are so romantically befuddled that they travel into the past for guidance, for example, Courtney in Laurie Viera Rigler's *Confessions of a Jane Austen Addict* (New York, Dutton, 2007) and Laurie Brown, *What Would Jane Austen Do?* (Naperville, Sourcebooks Casablanca, 2009). Much the same can be said of the television series *Lost in Austen,* in which Amanda Price steps into the novel *Pride and Prejudice* in search of the right man, Fitzwilliam Darcy (director: Dan Zeff; script: Guy Andrews; starring, Jemima Rooper, Elliot Cowan, Hugh Bonneville, 2008).

8 See Caroline J. Smith's analysis in *Cosmopolitan Culture and Consumerism in Chick Lit* (New York and London, Routledge, 2008), 12–13.

9 A good example would be *Sex and the City* where the main protagonist, Carrie Bradshaw, writes newspaper columns about relationships, fashion, and women's issues, centred on her relationship with her three close female friends. See *Sex and the City* (creator: Darren Star, based on the novel *Sex and the City* by Candace Bushnell, starring Sarah Jessica Parker, Kristin Davis, Cynthia Nixo, and Kim Cattrall, 1998–2004).

10 A question which many readers, who are interested in the chick lit genre, could be asking

Fielding's story, is based on the eponymous hero of Austen's novel, a major source of the Austen-related culture that sprang up following the popular *Pride and Prejudice* BBC mini-series (Simon Langton, 1995), in which Colin Firth's Darcy became every woman's darling. It might be argued that Firth, Jennifer Ehle – in her role as Elizabeth Bennet – along with the writer Andrew Davies, directly and indirectly started a new women's genre in Western culture, a genre of comical narratives influenced by Austen, where heroines seek Mr Right, with an additional emphasis on the daily struggles of women.[11]

Helen Fielding "borrows" the main plot from the television series rather than from Austen's actual work[12] even having Bridget watch the series in the first novel.[13] Even though *Bridget Jones's Diary* is the best-known modern adaptation of *Pride and Prejudice,* Austen's world is never very far away from the general chick lit narrative, as is shown by the fact that one of the many books written about the genre, an introduction in creative writing, is named in her honour: *See Jane Write. A Girl's Guide to Writing Chick Lit.*[14]

Chick lit novels tell us a good deal about the many issues facing modern women and their status in society; they shed light on women's self-image, race, social class, and femininity. However, most novels within the genre have a limited perspective on the world because they usually depict women who are white, single, and straight, in their twenties and thirties, living in cities and fending for themselves. Chick lit heroines are sexual beings and usually have several sexual

---

themselves is whether chick lit is still a genre? Laura Miller asks whether chick lit is dead in her article published in 2012 claiming that "its heyday has definitely passed". Heike Mißler quotes an editor at Kensington Publishing Corporation who says that they have "pretty much stopped publishing chick lit." See Heike Mißler, *The Cultural Politics of Chick Lit: Popular Fiction, Postfeminism, and Representation* (London/New York: Routledge, 2017), 12 and Laura Miller, "The death of chick lit", *Salon* (February 23rd, 2012). https://www.salon.com/2012/02/23/the_death_of_chick_lit/ Accessed Nov. 2023.

11 Austen has also been associated with Candace Bushnell, the other major foremother of chick lit, whose most famous work, *Sex and the City*, has been described as "Jane Austen with a martini". Candace Bushnell, *Sex and the City* [1996] (London: Abacus, 2010). Text on front cover.

12 Helen Fielding has described how the *Pride and Prejudice* mini-series helped her formulate the story of Bridget Jones. She had written a collection of stories for her column but lacked an overall plot. At that time the series was being shown by the BBC, and it completely captivated her, so she decided to "steal the plot". See "Bridget Jones vs Pride and Prejudice", *BBC*, "News, Entertainment & Arts", January 28th 2013, http://www.bbc.co.uk/news/entertainment-arts-21204956. Accessed Nov. 2023.

13 Helen Fielding, *Bridget Jones's Diary* (London and New York: Viking, 1996), 215. Harzewski stresses the tragic sides of Bridget and says that despite the obvious intertextuality with Austen, "Bridget is very much her own character" and that she is "more of a humorous creation than a heroine of emulation". See Stephanie Harzewski, *Chick Lit and Postfeminism* (Charlottesville/London: University of Virginia Press, 2011), epub, loc 53.

14 Sarah Mlynowski and Farrin Jacobs, *See Jane Write. A Girl's Guide to Writing Chick Lit*, Philadelphia (PA: Quirk Books, 2006).

partners, as is reflected in the television show *Sex and the City.* Rochelle Mabry argues that because the women in *Sex and the City* are so candid about sex, they represent contemporary women who want to investigate the mysteries of modern sexual relationships and gender roles on their own terms,[15] employing techniques that make them feminine, very much like the so-called Woman's films of the 1930s and 1940s did, which were motivated by a female point of view and used devices such as voice-overs, flashbacks, and fantasy sequences to give the female protagonist a voice and to emphasize that this is her story.[16] Contemporary novels, films, and television shows, like romance novels and older forms of women's films, tend to present a conservative image of women and their place in society. However, the chick lit stories also point to an important shift in the way women's experiences and desires are examined. The novels give modern women a voice, and "allow them to express desires that may lie outside the "happy-ever-after" marriage to Prince Charming."[17]

As Juliette Wells has described, these novels focus on the same temptations that fascinated Virginia Woolf when walking the streets of London.[18] Although most chick lit novels lack the poetry of Woolf's description, all these shoes, gloves, and scarves described by her in *A Room of One's Own*, give an idea of feminine beauty ideals, female vanity, and "plainness", which are preoccupations of chick lit. They imply that consumption may not always bring happiness, but that happiness can hardly be found without being a consumer of beauty in the widest sense of the word.[19]

Wells traces the subject matter of chick lit back to the eighteenth and nineteenth centuries, to Jane Austen and Charlotte Brontë. Austen was one of the first female authors effectively to tackle the female experience, as Deborah Kaplan has emphasised in her essential study, *Jane Austen Among Women,* which manifests Austen's importance to eighteenth-century women's culture, the context of the author's novels within a neglected and "insignificant" female reality."[20] As a response to such accusations, where the male eye defines literary

15 A. Mabry Rochelle Mabry, "About a Girl: Female Subjectivity and Sexuality in Contemporary 'Chick' Culture", *Chick Lit: The New Woman's Fiction*, 199–200.

16 Ibid, 195.

17 Ibid, 192.

18 See Juliette Wells, "Mothers of Chick Lit? Women Writers, Readers, and Literary History", *Chick Lit: The New Woman's Fiction*, 61–62. See also Virginia Woolf, *A Room of One's Own* (New York/London: A Harvest Book, 1981), 90.

19 It is worth mentioning that the first scene in the film *Pride and Prejudice* from 1940 takes place in a shop that sells linen clothing. Shopping thus becomes a part of the narrative in adaptations of the novel. See *Pride and Prejudice* (1940) (director: Robert Z. Leonard; scriptwriter: Aldous Huxley; producer: Hunt Stromberg; leading roles: Greer Garson and Laurence Olivier).

20 Deborah Kaplan, *Jane Austen Among Women* (Baltimore/London: The Johns Hopkins University Press, 1992), 85.

merit, one must keep in mind that Austen herself wrote within a "meaningless" female sphere where women's voices were seldom heard, and their everyday lives and feelings were overlooked. This is an old saying that has been repeated throughout the reception history of women's writing and is clearly illustrated through the reception history of Jane Austen's novels in the 19th and the early 20th century. She was criticized for depicting the mundane, everyday life of the landed gentry during one of the most eventful periods of European history: the Napoleonic Wars.[21]

Austen's focus on the daily lives of women has given her the reputation of being deeply absorbed in domestic and material detail. Wells emphasizes though that scenes of shopping are relatively few in Austen's novels (characters sometimes purchase ribbons and gloves) and that she usually describes clothing or jewellery only for satirical purposes.[22] Cathy Yardley's textbook for aspiring chick lit novelists, *Will Write for Shoes: How to Write a Chick Lit Novel*,[23] playfully captures this characteristic fashion-consciousness of the genre, which is often ironic and depicted in a humorous light. The chick lit heroine is dominated by an obsession with her looks and appearance, and publishers sometimes exploit this obsession by using purses and shopping bags as their imprint logo.[24] The genre is closely related to commercialism and consumerism, and Harzewski has pointed out notable parallels between the genre's reception history and the censure surrounding early English novels at a time when reading romance novels was considered pathological and associated with women's rabid appetite for new fashions.[25]

This emphasis on consumption in contemporary fiction is possibly most obvious in Kinsella's *Shopaholic* series and plays a big role in the ways these novels were marketed. The heroine's self-image is shaped almost exclusively by her purchases, financial status, and love life, the genre distinctively combining

---

21 See a thorough chapter on the reception history of Jane Austen in Emily Auerbach, *Searching for Jane Austen* (London: The University of Wisconsin Press, 2004), 27–36. See here especially Auerbach's discussion on the uneventful life of Jane Austen. A survey from 1912 "listed Austen as a "good looking, sociable maiden aunt" utterly removed from current events: "For her there existed no French Revolution, no public abuses, no history."" See Auerbach, 27. See also Oliver Elton, *Survey of Literature, 1780–1830:*1 (London: Edward Arnold, 1912), 191–92.

22 Juliette Wells, "Mothers of Chick Lit? Women Writers, Readers, and Literary History", 62–63.

23 Cathy Yardley, *Will Write for Shoes: How to Write a Chick Lit Novel* (New York: Thomas Dunne Books), 2006.

24 The Harlequin Red Dress Ink operated between 2004 and 2014, suggesting that the publishing house has since moved on to other labels in their marketing of women's fiction. See further discussion on the marketing of chick lit, Stephanie Harzewski, "Tradition and Displacement in the New Novel of Manners", *Chick Lit: The New Woman's Fiction*, 35. See also Harzewski's book *Chick Lit and Postfeminism*, epub, loc 31.

25 Stephanie Harzewski, "Tradition and Displacement in the New Novel of Manners", 35.

consumption with romance in the mind of the reader,[26] although it can be argued that the ironic style and various plot twists create anti-capitalist messages without rejecting the heroine. Austen's novels, however, are as preoccupied with behaviour, manners, and demeanour as chick lit novels whose heroines read glossy magazines and self-help books, the purpose being in both cases to guide women in their everyday lives, as well as create a comical atmosphere. Only time will judge the literary merit of chick lit, but it is obvious that the genre plays an important role in the history of women's writing.[27]

"I never saw such a woman." Austen's heroines, education, and feminine virtues

Mary Poovey focuses on the ideology that dictated female behaviour in the late eighteenth and early nineteenth century in her book *The Proper Lady and the Woman Writer.* The Proper Lady was supposed to have a comforting, restorative presence and to subordinate her needs to the will of her master, who was either her husband or her father. A good wife should not have an image of her own but must be like a mirror that reflects the face that looks into it, her needs and desires were defined by her husband.[28] This concept of female desire was not formulated solely by men, as some women even maintained that desire did not originate in a woman's emotions, imagination, or body. According to this ideology, the Proper Lady was governed by modesty. She did not love before marriage, but after she was married to her husband, she loved him for the rest of her life.[29]

Such was the fear of female sexuality by the late eighteenth century that women were advised not to allow or admit to themselves appetites of any kind that suggested enthusiasm.[30] They were encouraged to display no vanity, no pas-

26 Jessica Van Slooten, "Fashionably Indebted: Conspicuous Consumption, Fashion and Romance in Sophie Kinsella's Shopaholic Trilogy", *Chick Lit: The New Woman's Fiction*, 237.

27 In 2019, BBC named the stories about Harry Potter and Bridget Jones as "two of the most important English language novels, sitting alongside classics such as Pride and Prejudice and Middlemarch." See Laura Hampson, "Harry Potter and Bridget Jones named as 'most important' English novels", *The Standard* (Nov. 5th, 2019). https://www.standard.co.uk/culture/books/bbc-100-most-important-english-language-novels-a4279466.html. Accessed Nov. 2023.

28 Mary Poovey, *The Proper Lady and the Woman Writer: Ideology as Style in the Works of Mary Wollstonecraft, Mary Shelley, and Jane Austen* (Chicago/London: The University of Chicago Press, 1984), 3.

29 Ibid, 4.

30 Ibid, 5. Although conduct books greatly emphasized sexual chastity in women, sexual promiscuity was rife in high society during the Regency period. Venetia Murray writes that noblemen often had multiple mistresses who were respected in society. George III had sons who served as prototypes: the princes had wealthy mistresses who were often given respectable

sion, and no indication that they could conclude on their own. Women were thus urged to avoid all behaviour that would bring attention to themselves. One of the greatest compliments a woman could receive was not being talked about. Modesty was one of the most highly regarded feminine virtues because it gave a clear indication that a woman could control her sexual appetite and ensured protection against male importunity.[31] Modesty was also a sign of purity: it promised fidelity in a wife and reflected the husband's power over her. A bold woman made a show of herself while a woman who was modest called attention to her husband by reflecting his gaze back at him. It was not considered appropriate for women to initiate conversations at social gatherings: they were expected to use facial expressions to convey their opinions.[32] The man sees his reflection in the void that is the woman and realizes the power he has over her: "The woman as desiring subject is "blackness", a cultural void, a negative that comes into view only when it interferes with the ideal woman, who cannot be seen at all."[33] The paradox of this ideology is that modesty and innocence were simultaneously meant to make a woman attractive and desirable as a partner; the innocence shown in her behaviour was thus a sign of her hidden sexuality's potential. She could therefore never be truly innocent for she would always unintentionally betray the sexuality that her virtue exists to protect.[34]

Austen's heroines generally do not fit the perfect image of femininity depicted in contemporary conduct books, just as the chick lit heroines do not represent the values seen by modern femininity as desirable. Emily Auerbach points out that in Elizabeth Bennet, Austen presented a female character who was dramatically different from any other female character that had previously appeared in English fiction.[35] Austen herself claimed that there had never been a heroine like Elizabeth, calling her "as delightful a creature as ever appeared in print" and

titles. Some even had more significant roles in their lives than the wives. Royal bastards had a status of their own and the sons were even given titles. see Venetia Murray, *High Society in the Regency Period 1788–1830* (London: Penguin Books, 1998), 134–135. Roy Porter also points out that although affairs were usually kept secret, they were considered acceptable by high society. Noblewomen were sexually active, and many had sexual partners outside of marriage. Many women felt better off being kept as mistresses than being servants or wives of poor men. Famous mistresses such as Grace Dalrymple Elliott and Fanny Murray enjoyed respect and fame. Men in public life were commonly seen out and about with their mistresses and sometimes even married them. Although there was still a stigma around illegitimate children, high society often overlooked it, and bastards were sometimes raised alongside legitimate children. See Roy Porter, *English Society in the 18th Century* (London: Penguin Books, 1990), 261–263).

31 Mary Poovey, *The Proper Lady and the Woman Writer*, 21.

32 Ibid, 24.

33 Ibid, 22.

34 Ibid, 26.

35 Emily Auerbach, *Searching for Jane Austen*, 129.

doubting whether she could tolerate anyone who did not like her.[36] Elizabeth speaks in a lively manner, she likes making puns, twisting words, and debating with people. At the same time, she develops throughout the story as she proceeds from disliking the hero to falling in love with him. It is not her appearance that initially attracts Darcy to Elizabeth, nor is it a display of any of the traditional contemporary feminine virtues such as those detailed by Poovey: virtues such as modesty, humility, or submissiveness. It soon becomes clear to the reader that Elizabeth is anything but dispassionate, opinionless, or unconscious of her sexuality.

Austen nonetheless engages in purposeful dialogue with contemporary conduct books in her novels, though she uses them as a source of humour as well as giving them serious treatment. This is evident when Mr. Collins is proposing to Elizabeth. In this scene, Austen is intentionally playing with contemporary archetypes of modesty and mocking them. When Elizabeth makes it clear that she does not wish to speak privately with Mr. Collins, he interprets this as modesty and natural delicacy on her part, and adds: "you would have been less amiable in my eyes had there *not* been this little unwillingness."[37] When Elizabeth repeatedly rejects his proposal, he takes it as a sign of outward modesty and believes that she is flirting with him: "… and perhaps you have even now said as much to encourage my suit as would be consistent with the true delicacy of the female character."[38] Mr. Collins purposely attributes her response to a "wish of increasing [his] love by suspense."[39]

Pride and Prejudice can be read as a story about manners and social behaviour. These two subjects shed light on the class system of Austen's times and can in some cases be an important key to her characters. This is especially apparent in her description of the pretentious, extremely courteous, and arrogant Mr. Collins who it seems has pored over conduct books since childhood. Judging by Mr. Collins, one might assume that the reading of such books is not meaningful in itself, because the reader must possess the ability to evaluate their moral message if they are to be useful. Mr. Collins' manner is characterized by a strange mixture of "pride and obsequiousness, self-importance and humility."[40] Penelope Joan Fritzer points out that in her rendering of Mr. Collins, Austen is

36 *Jane Austen's Letters*, "To Cassandra Austen", January 29th 1813, *Jane Austen's Letters*, ed. Deirdre Le Faye (Oxford/New York: Oxford University Press, 1995), 201: "how I shall be able to tolerate those who do not like *her* at least, I do not know."

37 Jane Austen, *Pride and Prejudice* (London: Penguin Books, 1996), 88–89: "Believe me, my dear Miss Elizabeth, that your modesty, so far from doing you any disservice, rather adds to your other perfections. You would have been less amiable in my eyes had there *not* been this little unwillingness […]."

38 Ibid, 91.

39 Ibid.

40 Ibid, 61.

making fun of the style recommended by conduct books.[41] He bows and scrapes to people in higher positions than his own but has no natural sense of what is appropriate behaviour. He is a flatterer, and in him "there is a mixture of servility and self-importance […]. His air was grave and stately, and his manners were very formal."[42] It is tempting to interpret the rendering of Mr. Collins as a parody of conduct books, as Austen is making fun of desirable characteristics such as politeness, respect, humility, and modesty by showing largely negative and shallow representations of them, as well as emphasising that her heroine has determination.

The Austen heroines' drive is a quality they share with chick lit heroines who, despite everything, are also kind-hearted and proud, and good and reliable friends, with qualities that cannot be learned online or in glossy magazines. The heroine is often compared with another woman, and the comparison sheds light on her positive qualities. Thus, Elizabeth differs from her more desirable sister character, Jane, in more than just words and gestures. Her behaviour is in many ways different from what contemporary conduct books recommend for young women. Elizabeth is cheerful and dynamic: and she talks back, making her the opposite of the ideal woman who does not show too much personality. Elizabeth is very physically active in the novel, and this signals her vitality: she is often depicted running through the countryside with ruddy cheeks and wearing a dirty dress and dirty shoes. Her physical activity is a major topic of discussion in an interview with Andrew Davies, the scriptwriter of the 1995 BBC series *Pride and Prejudice*, about the script and characters. Davies thinks that Elizabeth's ease of manner indirectly suggests sexual energy, which is what attracts Darcy to her: "[S]he is a very active, lively girl, not just mentally but also physically […]. I almost think that this is a coded way of Jane Austen telling us she's got lots of sexual energy. This is probably what appeals to Darcy, unconsciously at any rate, who is used to some very artificial females."[43] This famous television series describes a woman who is not afraid to show it off. Elizabeth is thus physically expressing herself in a way that is at odds with exemplary female behaviour of the time.

It is important to mention that there were differences in emphasis among contemporary conduct books, as Penelope Fritzer points out in *Jane Austen and Eighteenth-Century Courtesy Books.* Some works focused on good character rather than knowledge, others advised against education, and still others advocated breadth of learning.[44] Fritzer mentions *The Lady's Preceptor* and *The*

41 Penelope Joan Fritzer, *Jane Austen and Eighteenth-Century Courtesy Books* (London and Westport, Connecticut: Greenwood Press, 1997), 70.

42 Jane Austen, *Pride and Prejudice*, 56 and 57.

43 Sue Birtwistle and Susie Conklin, *The Making of Pride and Prejudice* (London: Penguin Books, 1995), 4.

44 Penelope Joan Fritzer, *Jane Austen and Eighteenth-Century Courtesy Books*, 9.

Whole Duty of Woman as two examples of conduct books that advised against the education of young women. She quotes the following from *The Whole Duty of Woman:* "for happier is she who but knoweth a little, than she who is acquainted with too much."[45] This, however, was not always the case. Some eighteenth-century conduct books encouraged the education of young women; Lady Sarah Pennington, for example, gives the following advice in her book *An Unfortunate Mother's Advice to Her Absent* Daughters: *In a Letter to Miss Pennington*

> study your own language thoroughly, that you may speak correctly, and write grammatically… French you ought to be as well acquainted with as English; and Italian might, without much difficulty, be added. Acquire a good knowledge of History – that of your own country first, then of the other European nations … Learn so much of Geography, as to form a just idea of the situation of places.[46]

Thus some eighteenth-century conduct books also emphasized language learning, writing, history, and reading. They all agreed that some basic education skills were necessary.[47] At the beginning of the nineteenth century, middle-class women were expected to know about playing the piano, drawing, French, grammar, geography, arithmetic, reading books, and needlework.[48] Fritzer writes that Austen's young female characters generally exhibit traits idealized by the authors of conduct books. Her foolish and witless female characters are talentless and lazy while the female characters that we admire are naturally talented. Austen holds housework in high regard and her good female characters (and some of her bad ones) are all hard-working.[49] This thesis conflicts with the view that all of Austen's female characters are hard-working or talented, since Austen herself emphasises through her novels that some were lazy rather than industrious, most notably Emma Woodhouse, Catherine Morland, and Elizabeth Bennet. However, Elizabeth possesses a wisdom that distinguishes her from her sister-characters. It cannot be said of any of her heroines that they are held in high regard for their industriousness, and none of Austen's heroines are so accomplished that they stand out among their peers.

In *Pride and Prejudice*, Austen mocks these highly idealized expectations of accomplished ladies: a knowledge of several languages, a talent for drawing, the playing of musical instruments, great conversation skills, and so forth. In the scene where Mr Bingley, Mrs Bingley, and Mr Darcy are discussing the education of women, Darcy claims that he "cannot boast of knowing more than half-a-

45 Ibid, 10.

46 Quoted in Penelope Joan Fritzer, *Jane Austen and Eighteenth-Century Courtesy Books*, 10.

47 Ibid, 12.

48 Leonore Davidoff and Catherine Hall, *Family Fortunes: Men and Women of the English Middle Class 1780–1850* (London and New York: Routledge, 2002), 289–290.

49 Penelope Joan Fritzer, *Jane Austen and Eighteenth-Century Courtesy Books*, 22–23.

dozen [women], in the whole of [his] acquaintance, that are really accomplished." Mrs. Bingley agrees with him and adds:

> no one can be really esteemed accomplished, who does not greatly surpass what is usually met with. A woman must have a thorough knowledge of music, singing, drawing, dancing, and the modern languages, to deserve the word; and besides all this, she must possess a certain something in her air and manner of walking, the tone of her voice, her address and expressions, or the word will be but half-deserved.[50]

To this, Darcy replies: "All this she must possess [...] and to all this she must yet add something more substantial, in the improvement of her mind by extensive reading." Elizabeth's response makes it clear that no woman can meet such demands: "I am no longer surprised at your knowing *only* six accomplished women. I rather wonder now at your knowing *any.* [...] I never saw such a woman. I never saw such capacity, and taste, and application, and elegance, as you describe, united."[51] Their conversation emphasizes that Austen was not trying to describe an ideal eighteenth- or nineteenth-century woman but rather a real woman who, despite her flaws, has special traits and something unique to offer.

Fritzer points out that Elizabeth received a liberal education advised by some contemporary conduct books, such as *Universal Mentor.* Through her education and her intelligent father, she is taught to view men as they are. It is for this reason that she can see right through Mr. Collins and eventually recognize the real Mr. Darcy hiding behind the cold mask.[52] Elizabeth, however, has a strong independent spirit and the reader will not accept that her personality was wholly shaped by her father. He undoubtedly had a positive influence on her, but the novel implies that he was distant during her childhood and imposed few restraints on his children, particularly on his youngest daughter, the reckless Lydia. Austen thus deviates from contemporary conduct books, both those that advised little education and those that recommended a broad education. Education is certainly important for her female characters, but it does not occupy all their time, and they do not excel in desirable subjects such as drawing, singing, reading, playing music, or learning languages.

Similarly, Emma Woodhouse is unwilling to undergo the disciplinary process designed to prepare young women of high society for life, for she wishes neither to ennoble herself by practising art nor to receive an education. Despite this, she takes the orphan Harriet Smith under her wing and is resolved to introduce her to good society and to find her a husband of noble birth. She overestimates her matchmaking abilities, however, and leaves Harriet with unrealistic expectations and little hope of marrying the man who loves her. Emma has a comprehensive

50 Jane Austen, *Pride and Prejudice*, 35.

51 Ibid, 35–36.

52 Penelope Joan Fritzer, *Jane Austen and Eighteenth-Century Courtesy Books*, 11.

knowledge of social customs, just like contemporary chick lit heroines who pore over glossy magazines and self-help books in search of make-up tips, the latest fashion, or guidance for their daily life.[53] Society at large demands that women behave in a certain manner, and, just like the heroines of chick lit, Emma has difficulties abiding by these rules and customs. Emma is a good example of an Austen character who does not meet the socially accepted definition of an ideal nineteenth-century woman, despite being "handsome, clever and rich."[54] She is also the most flawed Austen protagonist in the moral sense of the word, and the only one who finds it hard to differentiate between right and wrong. Her behaviour is excused with the explanation that she has had no restraints imposed upon her: she always does just what she likes and, in most cases, follows her own judgment.[55]

Emma is frequently compared to Jane Fairfax in such a way as to bring out her flaws, partly to highlight the superiority of the latter. Jane is an orphan and the niece of Miss Bates. She is provided with an excellent education by her benefactors, Colonel Campbell and his wife (the element "fair" in her name is no coincidence). Emma is intelligent and she likes to draw, play the piano and sing, but she has neither practised as hard as Jane nor received the same education. This is most likely because Emma had to raise herself: "the real evils indeed of Emma's situation were the power of having rather too much her own way."[56] She grew up with a father who never saw any wrong in her so that few restraints were imposed upon her: "I do not know any body who draws so well as you do,"[57] says Mr Woodhouse to Emma, and adds "there is nobody half so attentive and civil as you are."[58] Mr Knightley is the only one who sees any faults in Emma giving him

53 Caroline J. Smith talks about how the producers of women's magazines rely on consumer culture. Even if the magazines encourage women to improve and better themselves they don't count on them succeeding or else "the consumer market for such publication would be in jeopardy". See *Cosmopolitan Culture and Consumerism in Chick Lit* (New York/London, Routledge, 2008), 21.

54 Jane Austen, *Emma* (London/New York: Penguin Books), 1996, 7.

55 Ibid, 7. Malcolm Bradbury says that the "artistic problem of the book" is to let us care for Emma and about her fate but without subduing our own "moral feelings about her faults". See his article "Jane Austen's Emma" in *Jane Austen: Emma*, ed. David Lodge (London: McMillan, 1968), 166. The writer Andrew Davies has voiced an interesting opinion on Emma which comes through in his adaptation from 1996 (starring Kate Beckinsale), where Emma's faults become apparent, the character lacking the warmth and softness which is also a part of her personality in the novel. "Emma Woodhouse is arrogant, ignorant, snobbish, a control freak, and a bully, who treats other people as if they were mechanical toys. She has little insight into others and almost no self-knowledge. […] In *Emma* the heroine is the Rich Bitch." See Andrew Davies: "Emma 3. Austen's horrible heroine." *Emma Adaptations.* https://www.strangegirl.com/emma/daviestel.php accessed Nov. 2023.

56 Jane Austen, *Emma*, 7.

57 Ibid, 42.

58 Ibid, 142.

status as both authority and at the same time a mentor or someone who simply encourages her to take on a more serious understanding of her role in society.[59] Jane Fairfax by comparison excels in many socially desirable qualities, which is the likeliest explanation of why Emma dislikes her: at one point she exclaims that "one is sick of the very name of Jane Fairfax."[60] This, at least, is the explanation given by Mr. Knightley who is certain that Emma is jealous of Jane because "she saw in her the really accomplished young woman, which she wanted to be thought herself."[61]

Austen uses certain words to describe Jane Fairfax that highlight her talents: sensitive features, a delicate nature, and tenderness; these were all considered highly desirable feminine traits during the Regency period. Jane is "accomplished and superior"; she has been "given an excellent education", and is superior to Mrs. Campbell "both in beauty and acquirements", she has "higher powers of mind", and is "elegant, remarkably elegant, graceful", an "elegant creature", and has "softness and delicacy in her skin which gave peculiar elegance to the character of her face."[62] Jane also has her flaws, however. She is characterized by "coldness and reserve", she is "so cold, so cautious" and "so very reserved",[63] and in comparing her with Emma the reader can see how warm, open, lively, and fun Emma is, despite lacking some of the characteristics idealized as perfect feminine virtues.

When Jane Fairfax sits down at the piano and starts singing, Emma admits that "both [her] vocal and instruments [...] [are] infinitely superior to her own." She regrets the inferiority of her own? playing and blames it on her undisciplined childhood. She decides to turn things around: "She did most heartily grieve over the idleness of her childhood - and sat down and practised vigorously an hour and a half." When Harriet praises them both for their musical abilities, Emma says to her: "Don't class us together, Harriet. My playing is no more like her's than a lamp is like sunshine."[64] Emma is fully aware that Jane Fairfax is superior to her in almost every desirable way, at least as a singer and piano player.

The basic irony of *Emma* is possibly to be found in the heroine herself. Emma has difficulties behaving according to ideal feminine expectations, yet she takes Harriet as protégée and tries to give her the much-needed sophistication that she has disregarded. Emma wants to teach Harriet good manners, improve her knowledge, and teach her how to form correct opinions: "*she* would notice her; she would improve her; she would detach her from her bad ac-

59 Ibid, 12.
60 Ibid, 74.
61 Ibid, 138.
62 Ibid, 88, 137, 139, 143, 165.
63 Ibid, 139, 140, 166.
64 Ibid, 188, 191.

quaintance, and introduce her into good society; she would form her opinions and her manners."[65] This does not go as planned, however, as Emma often cannot be bothered to teach Harriet or actively improve her knowledge, as with the reading of books:

> Her views of improving her little friend's mind, by a great deal of reading and conversation, had never yet led to more than a few first chapters, and the intention of going on to-morrow. It was much easier to chat than to study; much pleasanter to let her imagination range and work at Harriet's fortune, than to be labouring to enlarge her comprehension or exercise it on sober facts.[66]

Emma would rather let her mind wander and imagine that Harriet has aristocratic ancestry and that she will find her a worthy husband: "…that she is a gentleman's daughter, is indubitable to me",[67] says Emma, during an argument with Mr. Knightley after she has decided to prevent Harriet from marrying the farmer Robert Martin. She thus decides to focus on Harriet's possible blue blood and nobility instead of taking on the more difficult task of a complete makeover. Emma is governed primarily by her imagination and her attempts at matchmaking largely resemble the fantasies of Don Quixote in the eponymous novel by Miguel de Cervantes. She is deeply preoccupied with bending the reality of Highbury to make it follow the narrative principles of romance novels and is accustomed to having things her own way. Miss Taylor, her governess, never disciplined her and was more like a sister or a friend to her, as opposed to a teacher.[68]

As mentioned above, Austen's heroines do not comply with contemporary conduct books; they express opinions that are too strong, they are too independent and determined, or they have overactive imaginations that repeatedly get them into trouble. It is also often the case in chick lit novels that the heroines do not follow the unwritten rules of society when it comes to appropriate behaviour and often get themselves into situations they cannot easily handle.

65 Ibid, 22.
66 Ibid, 60.
67 Ibid, 54.
68 Ibid, 7. "[T]hey had been living together as friend and friend very mutually attached, and Emma doing just what she liked; highly esteeming Miss Taylor's judgement, but directed chiefly by her own".

"Like 'creative accounting'". Emma Woodhouse and Rebecca Bloomwood

The novel *Emma* is the only novel by Austen that bears the name of the protagonist, which is fitting, since the heroine is extremely self-centred. Emily Auerbach points out that Emma Woodhouse comes closest of Austen's heroines to exhibiting artistic powers, and that the authoress coined the word "imaginist" solely to describe her.[69] Like an author fired up by her task of creating characters and plots, Emma "goes to work [...] on the people around her, finding an escape from boredom."[70] She is governed by her imagination which often gets her into trouble and humorously describes herself as a "fanciful, troublesome creature!" with a "mind delighted with its own ideas."[71]

Emma sees Harriet as a blank slate: she is like an author shaping characters at her convenience and creating situations to suit her narrative thread. When Harriet first dines at Hartfield she immediately becomes obsessed with her and believes her to be the perfect subject for an exciting new project.[72] Harriet and her potential love affairs are arguably the main focal point of the stories that Emma likes to create. Still, her imagination takes off when she hears how Mr Dixon, Colonel Campbell's son-in-law, saved Jane Fairfax when she fell overboard on a boating trip off Weymouth. Emma particularly likes to create love stories: "One might guess twenty things without guessing exactly the right", she says when describing the imaginary love affair between Jane Fairfax and Mr Dixon to Frank Churchill: "And then, he saved her life. Did you ever hear of that? – A Waterparty; and by some accident she was falling overboard. He caught her."[73] Emma is delighted that Mr. Knightley allows himself to let his imagination wander when he points out to her that Frank Churchill and Jane Fairfax are possibly in a relationship. She does not take him seriously and instead takes it as a sign that Mr Knightley has also started spinning stories: "She was in gay spirits and would have prolonged the conversation, wanting to hear the particulars of his suspicions, every look described, and all the wheres and hows of a circumstance which highly entertained her: but his gaiety did not meet hers."[74]

Emma's imagination runs especially wild when Churchill saves Harriet from the gipsies and brings her back to Hartfield. She quickly spins an adventurous and romantic narrative out of the situation, as seen in one of her more notable reflections:

69 Emily Auerbach, *Searching for Jane Austen*, 202.
70 Ibid, 202.
71 Jane Austen, *Emma*, 11, 22.
72 Ibid, see 22.
73 Ibid, 180.
74 Ibid, 290.

> Could a linguist, could a grammarian, could even a mathematician have seen what she did, have witnessed their appearance together, and heard their history of it, without feeling that circumstances had been at work to make them peculiarly interesting to each other? How much must an imaginist, like herself, be on fire with speculation and foresight! – especially with such a ground-work of anticipation as her mind had already made.[75]

Emma is convinced that everybody, even linguists and mathematicians, must see and feel that it is impossible for this young man and this lovely woman not to fall deeply in love under circumstances such as these. It also cannot be denied that Emma resembles Shakespeare's sister in *A Room of One's Own* by Virginia Woolf in her immense talent for spinning the fates of her friends, as Emily Auerbach has pointed out. Emma is a gifted woman trapped in a stifling society. She is an intelligent, strong, and artistic woman living in an environment that has no incentive and no outlet for women to express their creative nature.[76]

Many chick lit novels focus on women living in modern consumer societies, but perhaps none so much as Sophie Kinsella's *Shopaholic* series, which now numbers ten novels,[77] and Emma Woodhouse resembles the heroine Rebecca Bloomwood, insofar as they are both governed by their imagination which repeatedly gets them into trouble. In a modern society, where women have more freedom than their predecessors could have dreamt of having, however, they must overcome obstacles different from those facing Austen's heroines. In the first novel, *The Secret Dreamworld of a Shopaholic*, Becky is living in a flat in London with her wealthy best friend and works as a financial journalist for the magazine *Successful Savings.* There is a very subtle irony in these novels, and Kinsella uses humour to describe her heroine's addiction to clothes and shopping: Becky lives well beyond her means and owes the bank six thousand pounds. The biggest irony is that Becky works as a financial adviser and by the end of the first novel gets a job working as one on a television show and is finally able to pay all her debts with her new salary. Becky sees no point in "listening at press conferences",[78] just as Emma does not see the point of practising on the piano or reading or engaging in any activity that requires self-discipline. She

75 Ibid, 277.

76 Emily Auerbach, *Searching for Jane Austen*, 207. Virginia Woolf imagines in *A Room of One's Own* that Shakespeare had a sister and then tells her tragic story." See Virginia Woolf, *A Room of One's Own,* 113. See also Tony Tanner's analyses of Emma's isolation, intelligence, and boredom, living in the claustrophobic environment of Highbury. Tony Tanner, *Jane Austen* (Cambridge: Harvard University Press, 1986), 176–182.

77 The *Shopaholic* series are: *The Secret Dreamworld of a Shopaholic* (2000), *Shopaholic Abroad* (2001), *Shopaholic Ties the Knot* (2002), *Shopaholic and Sister* (2004), *Shopaholic and Baby* (2007), *Mini Shopaholic* (2010), *Shopaholic to the Stars* (2015), *Shopaholic on Honeymoon* (2014), *Shopaholic to the Rescue* (2016) and *Christmas Shopaholic* (2019).

78 Sophie Kinsella, *Confessions of a Shopaholic* (London: Black Swan 2009 [2000]), 27.

hardly ever follows the news and barely takes notes when she needs to. She "can't relax"[79] because she is distracted by thoughts of shopping. Emma and Becky both live in their fantasy worlds: Becky's existence is governed by vanity and consumer addiction while Emma's existence is governed by fantasies about love.

Becky can think on her feet and there is a good example of this at the beginning of the first novel when she gets herself into trouble over a scarf. She spots a sale sign for an expensive scarf in a shop window and asks the attendant to reserve it for her because she has forgotten her credit card at work. She can withdraw one hundred pounds from her debit card but is still twenty pounds short. Luke Brandon (whom she does not really know) offers to lend her the twenty pounds after she makes up a story about needing the money so that she can buy the scarf as a present for her aunt who is in hospital. Brandon is the head of the largest PR firm in London, he has a very high IQ, and on top of everything else can "read minds."[80]

Becky and various other chick lit heroines thus resemble Emma Woodhouse, who repeatedly gets herself into trouble over her made-up stories. Emma lies to Harriet, for example, when she says that she does not have a plaster for Mr Elton when he cuts his finger, forcing Harriet to give him a piece of hers. Emma looks shamefaced when Harriet recalls this moment and admits that she had plenty in her pocket: "My dearest Harriet!", cried Emma, putting her hand before her face, and jumping up, "you make me more ashamed of myself than I can bear. [...] One of my senseless tricks! – I deserve to be under a continual blush all the rest of my life."[81]

Rebecca Bloomwood also repeatedly makes up lies to get herself out of trouble. At the beginning of the novel this is revealed in the letters that Becky has received from the bank: "I am sorry to hear that you have broken your leg" and "I am sorry to hear that you have glandular fever", writes the bank manager Derek Smeath, and adds in his third letter, "I am sorry to hear you are still suffering from acute agoraphobia."[82] Her lies about her aunt in a hospital immediately come back to haunt her when she bumps into Luke as she leaves the shop with her new scarf in a bag. Luke teasingly asks her about the present for her aunt. He admires Becky's generosity, says that her aunt must be a "stylish lady", and finally asks her name. Becky, meanwhile, becomes increasingly embarrassed: her cheeks "flame red", she repeatedly clears her throat, and she feels "paralyzed." She says that her aunt's name is "Ermintrude", and Luke sends her aunt his best

79 Ibid, 28.
80 Ibid, 25.
81 Jane Austen, *Emma*, 280.
82 Sophie Kinsella, *Confessions of a Shopaholic*, 10, 11, 320.

wishes.[83] Becky is caught in the lie again when she meets Luke at a restaurant wearing the scarf, where she is dining with her friends, as he is with his parents and makes up a quick story about how her aunt had died in a hospital when the doctors amputated her septic leg.[84]

Becky thus repeatedly creates an atmosphere with her lies that is simultaneously uncomfortable for her and comical for the reader; pretending to be accomplished, she lies that she is "fluent in Finnish"[85], in a job interview which gets her into serious trouble when she is scheduled for a meeting with the recruitment director of the Bank of Helsinki and is expected to speak Finnish. She also lies that Derek Smeath, the manager of Endwich Bank, is stalking her so that she will not have to answer his calls.[86] Becky's character flaws also work to her advantage as it is they which charm Luke Brandon who praises her for her "imagination."[87] Her response shows this other side of her having an overactive imagination: "That's good, isn't it? That's quite flattering [...]. Hang on. It's not some polite way of saying I'm stupid, is it? Or a liar? Like 'creative accounting.'"[88] The lies that Becky tells to hide her consumer addiction repeatedly come back to haunt her, they create funny, embarrassing moments and sometimes, as a result, undermine her self-esteem.

Both Becky's and Emma's actions, due to their lively imagination, lies, spins, and fantasies, have serious consequences for many, themselves as well as other characters. Harriet rejects a proposal from a man to whom she is attracted because Emma actively convinces her that she should instead marry a man from a noble background but this intervention could have had dire consequences for Harriet's life. Becky becomes a fraud as a financial advisor when her spending is revealed publicly in *Shopaholic Abroad.* Both Emma and Becky are searching for a deeper meaning, living a life perhaps devoid of profound purpose, in a society that doesn't meet their rich need for creativity.

In Emma's case, her lack of formal education and a proper career partly explains her need to play with people as if they were living puppets with strings she can pull in whatever direction that pleases her. Both women find an outlet for their boredom and alienation through their imagination and by making up stories which become their shield from the aggression they experience from a patriarchal society. Neither woman has a chance to develop her intellectual powers because of deeper forces in the community that have invisible control over their lives and identities, thus creating a destructive outlet for themselves as well as for

83 Ibid, 35.
84 Ibid, 90–91.
85 Ibid, 155.
86 Ibid, 224.
87 Sophie Kinsella, *Confessions of a Shopaholic*, 161.
88 Ibid.

their friends and family. Emma lives in a confined area of the romance, but instead of writing stories, she makes them real by playing with people in her surroundings. Becky equally lives in a world that controls women by convincing them that they are never enough, they need to be prettier, thinner, smarter, richer, younger, sexier, and have a brilliant career as well as a fulfilling dating life.

Chick lit heroines suffer because they fail to fulfil the unrealistic expectations that govern modern society, and they are sometimes lacking in social skills, either because they have put themselves in uncomfortable situations as a result of a misunderstanding or awkwardness, or simply because they have gatecrashed the world of the rich and exclusive. Austen's heroines are more independent and determined individuals with a stronger sense of their self-worth than the chick lit heroines. As a result, they choose their husbands wisely, selecting individuals who either possess moral excellence or surpass others in intelligence and constancy.

Chick lit narratives tend to dwell on the heroines' insecurities, damaged self-esteem, and feelings of failure, the heroines find it difficult to handle the social norms surrounding their conduct, behaviour, consumption, career choices, or motherhood. The stories describe women's botched attempts to conform to the demands imposed upon them by a society governed by unrealistic standards, just as Austen's heroines were confined to a narrow female sphere with limited possibilities for developing their skills and talents.

Conclusion

Austen's novels address manners, behaviour, and speculations on appearance just like chick lit novels, although the story settings and the scenes are very different. Austen's heroines show their independence by rejecting the conduct manuals of their times despite being at the same time influenced by them. In this, they differ from the heroines of chick lit who become more bewildered, confused, and alienated as they consume more of the self-help books that shape the modern female self, moulding their identity and relationships. In this, these contemporary characters are in sharp contrast to their much older counterparts who rest more easily in their faults, despite living in a society devoid of social rights for women.

Jimenez and Rice's influential study on self-help books from the eighties is interesting from this perspective, since these works transformed the culture that chick lit rose from. It reveals a reality that doubtless has influenced modern women's relationships with men. Their article "Popular Advice to Women: A Feminist Perspective", examines how feminist achievements are being eroded in the popular culture through self-help books for women. They emphasise that the main purpose of guidebooks aimed at them, whether or not they have a scientific basis, is to make women accept their place in the private sphere. This is accomplished by placing love on a pedestal and deeply linked with the expansion of the marketplace or public sphere, the governing principles of which are competition, individualism, and egocentrism.[89] Jimenez and Rice consider that the ballooning of self-help books in the eighties turned this particular literary genre into an important factor in the cultural excommunication of women. The main responsibilities of domesticity were once again placed in their hands, and they had to adapt their lives to altered circumstances, taking on the commitments of marriage and childbearing in addition to fanning the flame of the relationship.[90]

It is possible to argue that both Austen's novels and the chick lit genre are engaged in drawing out the tension between the private and public sphere, that Jimenez and Rice analyse, and Poovey and Fritzer describe in their books. The stories predict limited egress for their female heroines, the public sphere is still a reality they have minimal access to. The overriding cynicism that governs the works of chick lit authors such as Fielding and Kinsella, suggests that their heroines have not bettered themselves despite finding love and a man. Neither are they in a better relationship with themselves or their society.[91] This could also be said of some of Austen's novels, especially *Emma* and *Northanger Abbey*, where the heroines ward off boredom through their fantastic tales. Emma takes on a more sensible role as a leader of her society at the end of the novel but ironically, she must then end her relationship with Harriet, emphasising the firm hierarchy in the social structure, suggesting perhaps that Emma has to give up her vivid imagination, even her voice, to become a proper and respectful wife in Highbury.[92]

Thus, Austen undermines the happy ending for her heroine, since she will at the end of the novel walk straight into the claustrophobic and sterile world that

---

89 E.g. *Being a Woman: Fulfilling Your Femininity and Finding Love* (Toni Grant, 1988), *How to Make a Man Fall in Love with You* (Tracy Cabot, 1984), and *How to Keep a Man in Love with You Forever* (Tracy Cabot, 1986). See Mary Ann Jimenez and Susan Rice, "Popular Advice to Women: A Feminist Perspective", *Affilia* (5.3 1990), 23–24.

90 A prime example is *Being a Woman: Fulfilling Your Femininity and Finding Love* (1988) by Toni Grant. See Jimenez and Rice, "Popular Advice to Women: A Feminist Perspective", 20–21.

91 Rochelle Mabry points out that contemporary chick lit novels are as conservative as women's films, since the heroine is often silenced towards the end of the novel or film, as is seen in the final scene of the film adaption of *Bridget Jones's Diary* (2001), when Mark Darcy gives Bridget a new diary and she disowns her earlier writing. See A. Rochelle Mabry, "About a Girl: Female Subjectivity and Sexuality in Contemporary 'Chick' Culture", 205.

92 See *Emma*, 395: "Harriet, necessarily drawn away by her engagements with the Martins, was less and less at Hartfield; which was not to be regretted. – The intimacy between her and Emma must sink; their friendship must change into a calmer sort of goodwill; and fortunately what ought to be, and must be, seemed already beginning, and in the most gradual, natural manner."

she has for so long resisted. The discerning reader's only hope is that the heroine may find solace in the arms of a perfect gentleman who will support her in her newfound role. But that reality lies outside the realm of the story. Perhaps Austen is suggesting that the woman's voice is being suppressed from the moment she accepts her man's proposal, as is revealed in the proposal scene where the eloquent heroine of the novel loses her voice altogether. "What did she say? – Just what she ought, of course. A lady always does."[93]

93 Jane Austen, *Emma*, 354.

Sanna Schulte
(University of Vienna)

Oscillating to Decipher the World – On the Timeless Relevance of Early Romantic Irony

Abstract
How potent are the aesthetic concepts of romanticism, and what validity do they have beyond the epoch of Romanticism in literary attempts to decipher the world? Starting from this question, the transcendental poetry of romanticism and the principle of early romantic irony are at the centre of this essay. However, their significance extends beyond the romantic epoch, as shown by precursors such as Cervantes and postmodern authors whose poetological ideas are closely related to early romantic irony as defined by Friedrich Schlegel. On that basis, this thesis explores how the self-reflexive moments are a discussion of the conditions of the possibility of art and is the reason for the enduring fascination with romanticism. A possible explanation for the constant return to and renewal of romantic aesthetics over the course of literary history lies in romanticism's constant attempt to grasp the relationship between human existence and the world. In this respect, the romantic aesthetic conveys a sense of creation.

Keywords
Romanticism, Postmodernism, Irony, Italo Calvino, Friedrich Schlegel

The Romantic 'Potenzirung' of the Literary World

Die Welt muß romantisirt werden. …
Romantisiren ist nichts, als eine qualitative Potenzirung.[1]
(The world must be romanticized. …
Romanticizing is nothing but a qualitative realization of potential.)
Novalis

Novalis' dictum that the world must be romanticized through 'Potenzirung' (qualitative realization of potential) is one of the most accurate descriptions of the romantic relationship between perception of the world and poetry. The *mise en abyme*, the immensely popular romantic image within the image which is in-

1 Novalis, *Schriften. Die Werke Friedrich von Hardenbergs*, Bd. II (Stuttgart 1981), 545. Unless otherwise noted, all translations are my own.

finitely repeated, or mirrored, provides the vivid optical expression to this process. As an example of a literary version of *mise en abyme*, Italo Calvino suggests that the enchanting song of the sirens which Odysseus hears while tied to the ship's mast, tells his own story: the Odyssey.[2] Novalis' 'Potenzirung' can also be understood as a literary mandate to which poetics is bound. This concept recurs throughout the course of literary history and will be examined in more detail below.

This essay is divided into three parts. The first part provides an overview of established romantic research – with a focus on early romantic irony and its characteristic oscillation as primarily defined by Friedrich Schlegel. The first part also introduces the transcendental poetry of romanticism and the specific form of the arabesque and thus provides the theoretical framework for what Novalis calls 'Potenzirung'. The second part encompasses a wide range across space and time: from Shakespeare, Cervantes, and Sterne to postmodern authors such as Italo Calvino and Peter Handke. This section demonstrates how the presence of aesthetic principles articulated in early romanticism are present across epochs, languages, and national borders. The third, and last, part questions the reason for this apparent universality of aesthetic principles and seeks an answer in the early romantic aesthetics' ability to reflect on the conditions of possibility of art.[3]

On Romantic Aesthetics

With 'Ich bin mir selbst ein Gegenstand der Anschauung und des Denkens' (I am an object of contemplation and thought to myself), Immanuel Kant determines the principle of transcendental philosophy in his *Vorlesungen über Metaphysik* (*Lectures on Metaphysics*). This revolutionary philosophical perspective, which strives for self-consciousness, is transferred into a literary concept by the early romantics: They make themselves, their texts, and the conditions of literature the subject of their poetry. Reflections on the creative process of poetry, its structure, its models, and the desired effect on the reader all become the fulcrum of ro-

2 Italo Calvino, *Kybernetik und Gespenster. Überlegungen zu Literatur und Gesellschaft.* Aus dem Italienischen von Susanne Schoop (München/Wien 1984), 153–155.

3 This article allows me to take a very broad look back at my master's thesis on irony and reflection as narrative strategies of postmodernism, which was dedicated to Italo Calvino, Umberto Eco, and Peter Handke and their recourse to early romanticism and was written in 2009 at RWTH Aachen University under the supervision of Prof. Dr. Axel Gellhaus, who was later my doctoral supervisor. Revisiting this topic has reminded me of the conversations we had a long time ago and made me realize once again how important this discussion remains for me even after Axel Gellhaus's death. During our time together, a Gellhausian perspective has crept into my reading, my thinking, and my perception of the world, which continues to enrich my life to this day.

mantic literature. One reason for this focus on self-reflection lies in the fundamental questioning of the artistic process of creation by the Enlightenment. Where does literature come from, and on what conditions is it reliant when it is no longer determined externally? The early romantic poets and thinkers seek within themselves the circumstances of their creations and develop the concept of an autonomous and self-reflective art. Literature gains self-awareness.

Among the most important theorists of early romantic poetics is Friedrich Schlegel[4], who develops a concept of transcendental poetry based on Kant:

> Möglichkeitsbedingungen von Erkenntnis verbindet. Analog dazu wäre Transzendentalpoesie eine Poesie, die in den Darstellungsprozess selbst die Reflexion über ihre eigenen und spezifischen Möglichkeitsbedingungen integriert.[5]

> Transcendental philosophy in Kant's sense is a philosophy that consistently combines the process of cognition with reflection on the conditions of possibility of cognition. Analogously, transcendental poetry would be a poetry that integrates into the representation process itself the reflection on its own and specific conditions of possibility.

Linked to self-reference and awareness of one's own artificiality is the concept of *romantic irony*, which Friedrich Schlegel places at the centre of his thoughts and characterizes as a 'steten Wechsel von Selbstschöpfung und Selbstvernichtung'[6] ('continuously fluctuating between self-creation and self-destruction'[7]). For that which is created is constantly questioned and reflected upon, the possibility of its repeal always remains present.

> Das Absolute, das der Dichter aussagen soll, stellt sich ihm als ein unentwirrbares Chaos dar. Er kann die Ordnung des Universalen mit seinem begrenzten Intellekt nicht erfassen sondern immer nur vereinzelte Einblicke gewinnen. Dieses Bewußtsein macht ihn skeptisch gegenüber seinem eigenen Schaffen. Er überläßt sich nie ganz ohne Rückhalt seinem schöpferischen Enthusiasmus, sondern macht dessen Produkt stets

---

4 Schlegel's importance for the poetological foundations of romanticism can almost be considered commonplace. Nevertheless, it is remarkable that these early definitions of the "poetry of poetry" are unchallenged in their validity for the entire epoch – the view of itself and the characteristics of the time succeed in such a way that the academic view of romanticism still rightly draws on it today. The complexity and epochal relevance of Friedrich Schlegel as a person and of his texts is demonstrated not least by their permanent presence in this *Romantik – Journal for the Study of Romanticisms.* Cf. Andreas Hjort Møller, "Bards, Ballads, and Barbarians in Jena. Germanic Medivalism in the Early Works of Friedrich Schlegel", *Romantik – Journal for the Study of Romanticisms* (2019), Volume 08, 13–34. Jørgen Huggler, "Democracy, General Will, and Political Formation. Friedrich Schlegel's Critique and Reconstruction of the Concept of 'Republicanism'", *Romantik – Journal for the Study of Romanticisms* (2020), Volume 09, 59–74.

5 Monika Schmitz-Emans, *Einführung in die Literatur der Romantik* (Darmstadt 2004), 51.

6 Friedrich Schlegel, *Kritische Friedrich-Schlegel-Ausgabe.* Zweiter Band. (München 1967), 172.

7 Friedrich Schlegel, *Philosophical Fragments.* Translated by Peter Firchow. Foreword by Rodolphe Gasché (Minneapolis/London 1991), 24.

zum Objekt eines kritischen Bewußtseins. Darum nennt Schlegel die Ironie den 'steten Wechsel von Selbstschöpfung und Selbstvernichtung'.[8]

The absolute, which the poet is supposed to express, presents itself to him as an inextricable chaos. He cannot grasp the order of the universal with his limited intellect, but can only gain isolated insights. This consciousness makes him setical of his own creation. He never completely surrenders himself without reserve to his creative enthusiasm but always makes its product the object of a critical consciousness. Therefore, Schlegel calls irony the 'constant alternation of self-creation and self-destruction'.

Friedrich Schlegel defines irony as a movement between two fundamentally irreconcilable opposites such as the finite and the infinite, order and disorder. The point is not to merge or reconcile the opposites, but to move between the extremes, a state of suspension, an oscillation. 'Es ist gleich tödlich für den Geist, ein System zu haben und keins zu haben. Er wird sich wohl entschließen müssen, beides zu verbinden.'[9] (It is equally fatal for the mind to have a system and not to have one. He will have to decide to combine both.) In the ironic space everything becomes flexible and relativized in the sense that the opposite is already taken into account, but it is not destroyed or untrue:[10] 'Alles was etwas wert ist, muß zugleich dies sein und das Entgegengesetzte'[11] (Everything that is worth something must be this and the opposite at the same time). Reflection takes a central position, which 'als Grenzwerte einer oszillierenden Bewegung beide Momente aus sich selbst hervorbringt: den Schein eines Gegebenen und seine (ironische) Rücknahme'[12] (as the limit values of an oscillating movement produces both moments from within itself: the appearance of a given and its (ironic) repeal).

Early Romantic irony can be considered an aesthetic theory of relativity, according to Peter Szondi: 'Die romantische Ironie faßt die Realität als ein Vorläufiges auf und bringt ihrerseits nur Vorläufiges hervor'[13] (Romantic irony conceives of reality as something temporary and in turn only produces something temporary). It is not necessary to discard something in order to assert something

8 Walter Bausch, *Theorien des epischen Erzählens in der deutschen Frühromantik* (Bonn 1964), 114.

9 Schlegel, *Werke*, II, 173.

10 Cf. Beda Allemann, *Ironie und Dichtung* (Pfullingen 1956), 23.

11 Schlegel, *Werke*, II, 177. For the interpretation of the sentence, see also: Ernst Behler, "Die Theorie der romantischen Ironie im Lichte der handschriftlichen Fragmente Friedrich Schlegels" in *Zeitschrift für deutsche Philologie. Sonderheft zum 88. Band. Friedrich Schlegel und die Romantik*, 90–115, 112.

12 Axel Gellhaus, *Enthusiasmos und Kalkül. Reflexionen über den Ursprung der Dichtung* (München 1995), 13.

13 Peter Szondi, "Friedrich Schlegel und die romantische Ironie. Mit einer Beilage über Tiecks Komödien" in *Ironie als literarisches Phänomen*, ed. Hans-Egon Hass und Gustav-Adolf Mohrlüder (Köln 1973), 149–162, 157.

else. Opposites can stand side by side, do not exclude each other, but are also never final: 'Das Gesagte wird durch die Art, wie es gesagt wird, aufgehoben zugunsten eines anderen, dem das gleiche Schicksal blüht, nämlich, kaum gesagt, zugunsten eines dritten sich aufheben zu müssen.'[14] (What is said is negated by the way it is said in favour of another, which suffers the same fate, namely, hardly said, to have to negate itself in favour of a third.) This poetological process is based on the realization that truth and reality cannot be grasped, but one can only try to approach them. Through romantic and ironic storytelling, the reader is encouraged to constantly doubt the predictability and availability of the world together with the author. What ultimately results from this approach is primarily 'Einsicht in die Gebrechlichkeit der Welt'[15] (insight into the frailty of the world). Friedrich Schlegel not only connects his transcendental poetry with the central concept of early romantic irony, whose characteristic movement is embodied by the term 'Oszillieren' (oscillation), but also with the form of the arabesque. According to him, the arabesque is the suitable form for ironic storytelling, because it has 'das Geschick, Heterogenes und einander Widerstrebendes in ein formales, ästhetisches Beziehungsverhältnis zu setzen, ohne die Andersartigkeit harmonisierend aufzulösen'[16] (the skill of putting heterogeneous and opposing things into a formal, aesthetic relationship without dissolving the otherness into harmony).

The arabesque is disorder and order at the same time, it unites chaos and artificial order, as well as heterogeneity and unity according to Schlegel's guiding idea of oscillation. The chaos is an expression of an incomprehensible order in the world, it imitates chance, is life itself. Every arabesque contains a system forming the framework for theory, reflection, philosophy: '"wahre Arabesken" vereinigen den Roman und die Theorie des Romans.'[17] (true arabesques unite the novel and the theory of the novel). Thus, the novel of the novel is created, which combines both theory and practice as well as poetry and science.

> Was schließlich die Verschmelzung von Poesie und Philosophie im Roman betrifft, die Schlegel forderte, so waren seine diesbezüglichen Bemerkungen nicht divinatorisch, sondern historisch getreu; denn das 18. Jahrhundert ist ja das klassische Jahrhundert des philosophischen Romans. Man denke etwa an Voltaires Polemik gegen Leibniz im

14 Manfred Frank, *Einführung in die frühromantische Ästhetik. Vorlesungen* (Frankfurt am Main 1989) 311.

15 Iris Denneler, *Die Kehrseite der Vernunft. Zur Widersetzlichkeit der Literatur in Spätaufklärung und Romantik* (München 1996), 122.

16 Ingrid Oesterle, "Arabeske Umschrift, poetische Polemik und Mythos der Kunst. Spätromantisches Erzählen in Ludwig Tiecks Märchen-Novelle 'Das alte Buch und die Reise ins Blaue hinein'" in *Romantisches Erzählen*, ed. Gerhard Neumann (Würzburg 1995), 167–194, 181.

17 Karl Konrad Polheim, "Friedrich Schlegels 'Lucinde'" in *Zeitschrift für deutsche Philologie. Sonderheft zum 88. Band. Friedrich Schlegel und die Romantik*, 61–89, 73.

> *Candide*, an Diderots *Jacques le Fataliste*, an die Rolle, die Humes Philosophie im *Tristram Shandy* spielt.[18]

> As for the fusion of poetry and philosophy in the novel, which Schlegel demanded, his remarks in this regard were not divinatory, but accurate in history; for the 18th century is the classical century of the philosophical novel. Think, for example, of Voltaire's polemic against Leibniz in *Candide*, Diderot's *Jacques le Fataliste*, the role that Hume's philosophy plays in *Tristram Shandy.*

Being in the World and Standing Above the World at the Same Time

The following section on Ludwig Tieck and Jean Paul is intended to illustrate how these theoretical ideas are clearly reflected in some central texts of the epoch. In addition, a first bridge to postmodernism opens a view of the applicability of early romantic concepts beyond romanticism: The kinship between Jean Paul's and Italo Calvino's texts becomes evident.

Whether Tieck's plays can be considered an appropriate literary counterpart to Friedrich Schlegel's theory of romantic irony is hotly disputed in literary studies. While Beda Allemann argues that Tieck's understanding of irony is based on the banal misunderstanding that irony is the destruction of illusion,[19] Ingrid Strohschneider-Kohrs tries to prove that the irony in Tieck's comedies goes beyond pure illusion destruction and can be recognized as aesthetic intention and design principle.[20] Friedrich Schlegel himself praises Tieck's 'Sinn für Ironie' (sense of irony) – in *Sternbal* 'scheint der romantische Geist angenehm über sich selbst zu fantasieren'[21] ('the romantic spirit seems to be daydreaming pleasantly about itself'[22]) – so I would like to briefly discuss Tieck's comedy *Der Gestiefelte Kater* (*The Puss in Boots*) for illustrative purposes.

The framing plot of the fairy tale brought to the stage is a caricature of the audience – quite comparable to Peter Handke's *Publikumsbeschimpfungen* (*Offending the Audience*), with the difference, however, that Tieck, for safety's sake, mocks a fictional audience. The story of the Puss in Boots yields in favour of the 'Spielidee der Konfrontierung des Theaters mit dem Theater'[23] (game idea of confronting the theatre with the theatre) and stages the same as an answer to

18 Hans Eichner, "Thomas Mann und die deutsche Romantik" in *Das Nachleben der Romantik in der modernen deutschen Literatur. Die Vorträge des Zweiten Kolloquiums in Amherst/ Massachusetts*, ed. Wolfgang Paulsen (Heidelberg 1969), 152–176, 161.

19 Cf. Allemann, *Ironie und Dichtung*, 50.

20 Cf. Ingrid Strohschneider-Kohrs, *Die romantische Ironie in Theorie und Gestaltung* (Tübingen 1977), 316.

21 Schlegel, *Werke*, II, 245.

22 Schlegel, *Fragments*, 84.

23 Strohschneider-Kohrs, *Die romantische Ironie in Theorie und Gestaltung*, 301.

the question, 'ob nicht Kunstwerke existieren, bei denen Täuschung nicht die erste Bedingung, das Hauptgesetz ausmacht'[24] (whether there are not works of art where deception is not the first condition, the main law). The romantic 'Potenzirung' (qualitative realization of potential) becomes clearly visible in the self-awareness of the characters as actors, in which the early Romantic poets and thinkers' ironic relationship with the world is reflected: the connection of the 'In-der-Welt-Seins' (being-in-the-world) with the 'Über-der-Welt-Stehen'[25] (standing-above-the-world). The leap to the meta-level is initially to be understood as an elevation – in contrast to Novalis' concept of 'Logarythmisieren' (logarythmizing). As with the constant provisional nature of everything written a mathematical aspect of romantic 'Potenzirung' as exponentiation becomes evident. The image of the *mise en abyme* shows this vividly.

The awareness of oneself as a human being or, respectively, a character is based on this double view. On the one hand it spells out human entanglement with the world and on the other hand seeks the outside perspective on this limitation; not to negate the former, but to contrastingly give equal validity to both. The programmatic change of perspective between microscope and telescope, for example, enables Jean Paul's typical irony and is part of his poetological fundamental concept:

> Ich konnte nie mehr als drei Wege, glücklicher (nicht glücklich) zu werden, auskundschaften. Der erste, der in die Höhe geht, ist: so weit über das Gewölke des Lebens hinauszudringen, daß man die ganze äußere Welt mit ihren Wolfsgruben, Beinhäusern und Gewitterableitern von weitem unter seinen Füßen nur wie ein eingeschrumpftes Kindergärtchen liegen sieht. – Der zweite ist: – gerade herabzufallen ins Gärtchen und da sich so einheimisch in eine Furche einzunisten, daß, wenn man aus seinem warmen Lerchennest heraussieht, man ebenfalls keine Wolfsgruben, Beinhäuser und Stangen, sondern nur Ähren erblickt, deren jede für den Nestvogel ein Baum und ein Sonnen- und Regenschirm ist. – Der dritte endlich – den ich für den schwersten und klügsten halte – ist der, mit den beiden andern zu wechseln.[26]

> I could never detect more than three roads to being happier (not happy). The first one which rises is: surging high enough above life's clouds to behold from afar the whole external world, with its pitfalls, charnel houses, and storm conductors spread out below one's feet like a dwindled, little child's garden. – The second one is: dropping straight down into that little garden and nestling so snugly in a furrow there that, again peeping from one's cosy nest, one will not set eyes on pitfalls, charnel houses, and rods, but only spikes of corn, each of them being tree, umbrella, and sunshade in one to the fledgling. –

24 Ludwig Tieck, *Nachgelassene Schriften.* Band 2 (Leipzig 1855), 142.
25 Szondi, *Friedrich Schlegel und die romantische Ironie*, 159–160.
26 Jean Paul, *Werke* IV 7, 10f.

> And lastly, the third one – which I consider the most arduous one and the wisest – is to alternate the other two.[27]

Schlegel, who has also criticized Jean Paul, refers to Jean Paul's texts in the *Brief über den Roman* (*Letter about the Novel*) as 'die einzigen romantischen Erzeugnisse unseres unromantischen Zeitalters'[28] (the only romantic products of our unromantic age). This praise refers to Jean Paul's narrative strategies, mainly the ironic and the reflective passages of the narrator figures, which condense into an independent story of narration. This gives Jean Paul's texts the balance between self-creation and self-destruction that is so central to Schlegel. Jean Paul succeeds in blowing up the traditional novel form and still writing a novel ('die tradierte Romanform zu sprengen und dennoch einen Roman zu schreiben'[29]).

Jean Paul's relationship to the Romantics is divided. Unlike Tieck, who is often cited as a prime example of romanticism, he does not fit clearly into this epoch. Jean Paul's irony and his conception of the novel bring him close to early romanticism, but he consciously distances himself from other romantic tendencies. Along with Friedrich Hölderlin and Heinrich von Kleist, Jean Paul is one of those greats of this time. These poets do not commit to one direction but develop independently and draw from various currents. For Jean Paul, the ironic reflection on narratability enables an unconditional opening. The carnival of allusions and possibilities that results from this seems comparatively postmodern from today's perspective.

In addition to the depiction of scenes of reading and storytelling, one of Jean Paul's strongest narrative strategies is the direct interaction with the reader through which the reflection of storytelling unfolds as a dialogical game. Jean Paul's narrators claim that they write for the reader's pleasure; let the sun rise and set for his sake.[30] His narrators address the reader directly – they call him a friend – and the shared view of the narrated events make the reader an accomplice. Sometimes it is simply 'wir zwei, ich und der Leser'[31] (we two, me and the reader). Sometimes this intimate complicity is ironically contrasted with a larger reading community: 'die paar tausend Leser, die mit mir ins Fenster sehen'[32] (the few thousand readers who look in the window with me). Precisely because the roles

27 Jean Paul, *A Reader.* Edited by Timothy J. Casey. Translations by Erika Casey (Baltimore/London 1992), 54. (*Billet to My Friends* 'instead of a foreword' to *Quintus Fixlein*).

28 Schlegel, *Werke*, II, 330.

29 Bruno Hillebrand, *Theorie des Romans I. Von Heliodor bis Jean Paul* (München 1972), 173.

30 'Geh auf, schöner Himmelfahrts- und Hochzeitstag, und erfreue auch Leser!' (Arise, beautiful Ascension Day and wedding day, and delight readers too!) Jean Paul, *Werke.* Vierter Band. Kleinere erzählende Schriften (München 1960), 145.

31 Ibid, 133.

32 Jean Paul, *Werke*, IV, 152.

that the reader plays in the text constantly change, the reader develops as a character his own dynamics, and thus the reader as a character focuses the attention of the real reader to the role assigned to him. The relationship between narrator and reader can indeed transform. It suddenly tips from the cosy, domestic, storytelling scene – as caricatured by the grandfather in the armchair and in which, as in *Das Leben des vergnügten Schulmeisterlein Maria Wutz (Life of the Merry Masterkin Maria Wutz in Auenthal):* 'die Vorhänge zugezogen und die Schlafmützen aufgesetzt werden'[33] ('the curtains must be drawn and our night-caps donned'[34]) – into a power game that is reliant on the reader's dependence on the narrator's pleasure: 'Ich breche hier ab, weil ich noch überlegen will, ob ich seinen Hochzeitstag abzeichne oder nicht'[35] ('I am going to break off here as I wish to consider whether I shall depict the wedding day or not'[36]). The narrative situation in which the reader is now invited to make himself comfortable in order to experience and reflect on all possible roles of reading in the story – from passionate to academic to a true encounter between writers and readers – is recognizable as the concept behind one of the most important novels of postmodern literature, Italo Calvino's *Se una notte d'inverno un viaggiatore* (*If on a Winter's Night a Traveler*), with the following sentences:

> You are about to begin reading Italo Calvino's new novel "If on a Winter's Night a Traveler" Relax. Concentrate. Dispel every other thought. Let the world around you fade. Best to close the door; the TV is always on in the next room. [...] Find the most comfortable position: seated, stretched out, curled up, or lying flat [...]; having your feet up is the first condition for enjoying a read.[37]

The simplest trick to draw the reader's attention to the art of storytelling is to make him aware of his own dependence on the narrator; e.g., by the narrator conveying his feeling of reluctance and fatigue.[38] Making the narrative situation the subject of constant reflection leads to an arabesque double structure of the text. This is characteristic of almost all of Calvino's novels: In *Il cavaliere inesistente* (*The Nonexistent Knight*), the narrator, the nun Teodora is ordered by the head of the monastery to write, and Teodora describes writing as a torment. Her role as a

33 Jean Paul, *Werke.* Erster Band. Die unsichtbare Loge. Hesperus, 422.

34 Jean Paul, *A Reader,* 83.

35 Jean Paul, *Werke.* Erster Band. Die unsichtbare Loge. Hesperus, 446. This omnipotence of the narrator is often disguised as consideration for the reader: "Schon gestern wußt' ich's; aber ich wollte dem Leser, den ich von weitem darauf bereite, nichts von der traurigen Nachricht sagen" (I already knew it yesterday; but I did not want to tell the reader, whom I am preparing from afar, any of the sad news). Jean Paul, *Werke*, IV, 173.

36 Jean Paul, *A Reader,* 102.

37 Italo Calvino, *If on a Winter's Night a Traveler.* Translated from the Italian by William Weaver, S. 9.

38 Thomas Mann, who is regarded as an important ironist, also uses this device in *Bekenntnissen des Hochstaplers Felix Krull* (*The Confessions of Felix Krull*), for example.

nun in the secluded monastery also makes it difficult for her to imagine the world outside the monastery walls: 'What can a poor nun know about the world? ... God alone knows how I shall describe the battle, I who by God's grace, have always been apart from such matters ... – of battles, as I say, I know nothing.'[39] Or: 'This tale I have undertaken is even harder to write than I thought. Now it is my duty to describe that greatest of mortal follies, the passion of love, from which my wow, the cloister and my natural shyness have saved me till now'[40].

While the reader may suspect that one cannot believe everything the narrator says, this becomes clearly evident at the end of the novel when it turns out that the nun occasionally transforms herself into a knight and exchanges her cloistered life for life on the battlefield. The reader of Jean Paul knows this playful annoyance of an unreliable narrator all too well. For the sake of audacity, the narrator in *Hesperus*[41] tells him again in all clarity: 'Leser kann man nicht genug betrügen, und ein gescheiter Autor wird sie gern an seinem Arm in Mardereisen, Wolfgruben und Prellgarne geleiten'[42] (Readers cannot be deceived enough, and a clever author will gladly lead them by his arm into marten traps, wolf pits, and spring traps).

Irony as a Principle of World Literature

Early romantic irony is defined as a systematic; i.e., aesthetic reflection on the conditions of the possibility of literature. As an open game of world destruction and world creation, early romantic irony is a timeless design principle.[43] The question arises as to the extent to which the ironic self-consciousness of literary texts is a criterion for world literature that is applicable beyond the romantic epoch. This question is entirely in the spirit of the inventors of romantic irony, not only because their aesthetics reflect a fundamental relationship between man and world, but also because the romantics engage intensively with European literary history. They translate world literature from numerous languages and refer in their literary designs to authors such as Dante, William Shakespeare, Miguel de Cervantes, and Laurence Sterne.[44] In particular, *Don Quixote* and

39 Italo Calvino, The Nonexistent Knight. In: Our Ancestors, translated by Archibald Colquhoun with an introduction by the author (London 1980), 308.

40 Ibid, 326.

41 The full title is: *Hesperus oder 45 Hundposttage. Eine Lebensbeschreibung von Jean Paul* (*Hesperus or Forty-Five Dog-Post-Days*).

42 Jean Paul I, S. 662.

43 On the topicality of romanticism, see also Dieter Baensch, *Zur Modernität der Romantik* (Stuttgart 1977) und Wolfgang Paulsen, *Das Nachleben der Romantik in der modernen deutschen Literatur* (Heidelberg 1969).

44 These authors would probably be surprised to be described as ironic. Until the early romantic

Tristram Shandy can be considered decisive precursors of the phenomenon of literary irony. The following will primarily consider the function of Cervantes' famous *Don Quixote* as a role model for Schlegel's irony concept, as well as address postmodern successors to romantic irony. It is less about specific comparisons than about a general expansion of the validity of romantic poetics. Literature cannot permanently return to a state before the invention of its self-consciousness. It becomes apparent that the simultaneous being-in-the-world and standing-above-the-world as a structural principle is at least implicitly significant before romanticism (as a literary recipe for success).[45]

Already the foreword of *Don Quixote* is a parody of the genre of 'the foreword' and thus views itself ironically. The friend's advice on how to write a foreword can be read as a rejection of the foreword. It is a justification for the fact that forewords are actually superfluous and rather hinder the reader's access to the text. Schlegel's idea of oscillation becomes clear here as a counter movement inherent in the text. The possibilities of the foreword are treated here *ex negativo*. Finally, the foreword ends where it should have begun: after the friend's advice.[46] The foreword is – here in the expressive and comical translation by Ludwig Tieck – a 'Fopperei aller Kommentatoren und der ganzen Gattung von Kommentaren' (mockery of all commentators and the whole genre of comments) and 'die falsche und eitle "Notwendigkeit" gelehrter Zitate, Randglossen und Erläuterungen Lügen straft'[47] (refutes the false and vain "necessity" of scholarly quotations, marginal notes, and explanations). Similarly *Don Quixote* is a parody of the 'knight novels' of the time and has the explicit goal of 'das Ansehen und die Gunst zu zerstören, die die Ritterbücher in der Welt und bei der Masse genießen' (destroying the reputation and favour that the knight books enjoy in the world and among the masses) and 'das auf so schlechter Grundlage ruhende Gerüste jener Ritterbücher niederzureißen'[48] (tearing down the scaffolding of those knight books resting on such a bad foundation).

---

period and Friedrich Schlegel's new concept of irony, irony was exclusively a concept of rhetoric and not a stylistic device in literature. Cf. Ernst Behler: *Ironie und literarische Moderne* (Paderborn 1997), 8.

45 Björk – along with many other pop culture artists – also knows how to build on this recipe for success. The music video for her song *Bachelorette* questions the conditions of the creation process of an autobiographical book, on which the song is based, and even includes the process of rewriting.

46 Even *The Life and Opinions of Tristram Shandy, Gentleman* by Laurence Sterne, although the title announces a whole life, a biography, hardly gets beyond the birth and baptism of the gentleman.

47 Goffredo Commi, *Realität der irrealen Dichtung. Don Quijote und Dante* (Reinbek bei Hamburg 1964), 21.

48 Miguel de Cervantes Saavedra, *Leben und Taten des scharfsinnigen edlen Don Quixote von LaManche*. Übersetzt von Ludwig Tieck und illustriert von Gustav Doré, I, 9f.

Cervantes uses the structure of the knight novels as a template to let his hero experience the typical adventures of a knight, including genre-typical motifs such as the search for a bride. Numerous allusions to other texts perfect the parody and depict the knight's world self-reflexively as a world of literature. The structure of the knight novel genre is ironically adopted to use its common motifs playfully. This is an artifice that is perfected again in postmodernism as shown in the approach of the early novels by Peter Handke. *Die Hornissen* (*The Hornets*), *Der Hausierer* (*The Peddler*), *Die Angst des Tormanns beim Elfmeter* (*The Goalie's Anxiety at the Penalty Kick*), but also *Der kurze Brief zum langen Abschied* (*Short Letter, Long Farewell*) play with the structure of the crime novel in such a way that the writing method becomes the actual theme of the texts. This is particularly evident in *Der Hausierer*, whose chapters are each divided into a theoretical part for the schematic components of a murder story and then a practical part for the theory's execution, the story of the peddler. In one of his most important poetological essays *I Am an Inhabitant of the Ivory Tower*, Handke writes that he is always primarily concerned with the method and the ironic exposure of the texts' construction.[49] 'Die Methode der Geschichte ist für mich nur noch anwendbar als reflektierte Verneinung ihrer selbst: eine Geschichte zur Verhöhnung der Geschichte' (The method of the story is only applicable to me as a reflected negation of itself: a story to mock the story.)[50]

Similar to Handke's ironically reflective crime stories, Italo Calvino's fairy tales are reflections on fairy tales and Umberto Eco's *Il nome della rosa* (*The Name of the Rose*) is a meta narrative of the historical novel. The original genre is by no means destroyed but remains as a narrative. The genre rather experiences a 'Potenzirung' in the romantic sense. The awareness of the respective exposed narrative art serves to increase the enjoyment of the narrative all the same as the Duke and Duchess demonstrate in the second part of *Don Quixote.* Although Don Quixote's follies in respect to his immersion in reading may be considered a warning to the reader, they are equally an invitation to the reader to follow him into the world of his imagination. The Duke and Duchess, who have already read the first part of the novel and thus know Don Quixote's peculiarities, indulge both themselves and Don Quixote the pleasure of playing his game.[51]

With Cervantes, this equal relationship between author and reader becomes a game in which ways of encountering the world are investigated. Cervantes is mainly concerned that his story is recognized as a possible reality: While historiography writes about reality as it is, poetry writes about reality as it should

49 Cf. Peter Handke, *Ich bin ein Bewohner des Elfenbeinturms* (Frankfurt am Main 1972), 26.
50 Ibid.
51 Cf. Marika Müller, *Die Ironie. Kulturgeschichte und Textgestalt* (Würzburg 1995), 56.

have been or could have been, as stated in the novel.[52] Poetry thus becomes a game of probability with rules that it adheres to reality and to the possible[53] 'weil die Lüge desto besser ist, je wahrhaftiger sie scheint'[54] (because the better the lie the truer it seems). *Don Quixote* is not the only example of romantic and ironic storytelling before romanticism, although certainly one of the most important. The game played with the reader and his expectations of a certain genre can also be found comparatively in the works of Denis Diderot. The narrator in Diderot's *Jacques le fataliste et son maître* (*Jacques the Fatalist and his Master*) not only disappoints the reader in his reading expectation, but also openly addresses the reader's expectations in a condescending, lecturing tone:

> Now, Reader, if you're thinking that this horse is the horse that was stolen from Jacques's Master you'd be wrong. That's how it would happen in a novel sooner or later, in this way or in another. But this isn't a novel, as I think I've already told you and now repeat.[55]

By the narrator addressing the reader directly and questioning his own genre affiliation, he aims not only to disillusion the expectant reader but, moreover, to push a whole genre that is based on illusion to the point of absurdity. 'Der wahre Narr ist ... der sich in der Sicherheit traditioneller Romankünstlichkeit wähnende Leser'[56] (the true fool is ... the reader who fancies himself in the security of traditional novel artistry). In the playful dialogue with the reader, the narrator's conception of the genre is revealed: genre-specific deceptive manoeuvres are exposed. A "look behind the scenes" into the text's secret mechanism and hidden inner life is granted. With the admission of the text's artificiality, a reflective level is attained, but at the same time, the pact between author and reader based on complicity is renewed. The author shows the reader the strings controlling the puppets and involves him in his work. His machinations become transparent. That the romanticizing 'Potenzirung' means a re-enchantment of the world becomes clear here on a structural level. Here the promise of the blue flower and the 'open sesame' is fulfilled. The insight into the creation of the ironic texts suggests a notion of the creation of the world.

52 Cf. Cervantes, *Leben und Taten des scharfsinnigen edlen Don Quixote von LaMancha*, II, 31.

53 Cf. Jommi, *Realität der irrealen Dichtung*, S. 29.

54 Cervantes, *Leben und Taten des scharfsinnigen edlen Don Quixote von LaMancha*, II, 455.

55 Denis Diderot, *Jacques the Fatalist and his Master.* Translated with an Introduction and Notes by David Coward (Oxford 1999), 116.

56 Denis Warning, "Opposition und Kasus – Zur Leserrolle in Diderots 'Jaque le fataliste et son maître'" in *Rezeptionsästhetik* ed. Rainer Warning (München 1979), 467–493, 471.

Deciphering the World

The striking parallels of the texts quoted in the previous part from such different epochs arise from the fact that they begin with the text itself in their search for what holds the world together at its core ('was die Welt im Innersten zusammenhält'). They conjure up an event that results from the fictional output from their own writing process and, complementarily, from being read.[57] The recognizable narrative order, the arabesque interplay of diversity and unity, may not only be considered a pattern for the respective genre and style in each and every case, but also points suggestively beyond itself – as Handke writes – to a 'Muster für einen größeren, einen noch größeren, den größtmöglichen [Zusammenhang]'[58] (pattern for a larger, an even larger, the largest possible [context]). Literature must be romantic, says Handke, who is very aware of his kinship with the romantics or their (conditionally affiliated) contemporary Jean Paul: 'Jean Paul – das ist ein Vorfahre oder Vorgänger meiner Person oder ich bin ein Nachgeborener'[59] (Jean Paul – that is an ancestor or predecessor of my person or [in other words] I am a post-born).

The proximity of romantic and postmodern literature arises, among other things, from a historical situation – as a reaction to the Enlightenment and the violence of the French Revolution against its children, as well as to the failure of the ideologies of the 20th century and the Holocaust. Irony 'als Seele der arabesken Form'[60] (as the soul of the arabesque form) presents itself in the historical perspective as a demarcation from previous epochs and is a refusal of a uniform representation and a naive belief in progress. Postmodern literature, in the 'Zeitalter der transzendentalen Heimatlosigkeit'[61] (age of 'transcendental homelessness'[62]), is thrown back on the creative process itself and seeks a way out with the key of the romantic idea of the readability of the world. The processes of reading and writing become mirrors of reality. Precisely because they are characterized

57 Vgl. Wölfel, Kurt: Jean Paul-Studien. Hrsg. v. Bernhard Buschendorf. Frankfurt am Main 1989, S. 57.

58 Peter Handke, *Versuch über den geglückten Tag. Ein Wintertagtraum* (Frankfurt am Main 1991), 20.

59 Peter Handke in a TV-Interview, *Gero von Boehm begegnet Peter Handke*, aired on 3Sat, 25. 09.2008.

60 Schlegel, *Lucinde*, 71.

61 George Lukács, *Die Theorie des Romans. Ein geschichtsphilosophischer Versuch über die Formen der großen Epik* (Darmstadt 1987), 32. Fernando Pessoa describes this as a consequence of the loss of political, social, and religious illusions and ideologies: 'We lost all of this. We were born with none of these consolations' (Fernando Pessoa, *The Book of Disquiet*. Edited and translated by Richard Zenith (London 2001), 306.)

62 George Lukács, *The Theory of The Novel. A historico-philosophical essay on the forms of great epic literature.* Translated from the German by Anna Bostock (London 1971).

by the temporary nature of irony and the 'Denkhabitus der Paradoxierung'[63] (thinking habit of paradoxization) they become credible in this historical situation. Calvino formulates this as a postmodern relationship to the world as well as a literary mission: 'Die Welt ist nicht lesbar, aber wir müssen gleichwohl versuchen, sie zu entziffern'[64] (The world is not readable, but we must nevertheless try to decipher it).

Walter Benjamin has precisely captured in his essay *Der Begriff der Kunstkritik in der deutschen Romantik*[65] (*The Concept of Criticism in German Romanticism*) where the strength and the continual attraction of romantic aesthetics lie. Schlegel achieves, according to Benjamin, the freedom of art from aesthetic doctrines not through attempts at a definition of harmony, but through a focus on the work as a medium of reflection of the possibilities and conditions of art in general.[66] Thus, Benjamin not only accurately defines early romantic aesthetics, but also focuses precisely on the element that represents the connection between early romanticism and postmodernism. Regardless of the relevance of aesthetics for the two epochs, the above explanations on the timelessness of this aesthetics and its recognizability in Cervantes (and, also, Sterne, Shakespeare, or Boccaccio) have shown that the seemingly early romantic irony represents a much more far reaching concept. Following Benjamin's thoughts, one reason for this could be that the decomposition of form through irony hints at the meaning of art as a mirror of creation.

> Die Ironisierung der Darstellungsform ist gleichsam der Sturm, der den Vorhang vor der transzendentalen Ordnung der Kunst aufhebt und diese und in ihr das unmittelbare Bestehen des Werkes als ein Mysterium enthüllt.[67]

> The ironization of the representational form is, as it were, the storm blast that rises the curtain on the transcendental order of art, disclosing this order and in it the immediate existence of the work as a mystery.[68]

Irony aims at every form and every form thus becomes 'the victim of ironic decomposition' (das Opfer der ironischen Zersetzung). Irony becomes the instrument to open to the absolute per se as it breaks with every uniform representation. Irony itself means – as in Schlegel's *Lucinde* – the transcendence of form. A

63 Gabriele Ines Betyna, *Kritik, Reflexion und Ironie. Frühromantische Ästhetik und die Selbstreferenzialität moderner Prosa. Thomas Bernhard, Peter Handke und Botho Strauß* (Düsseldorf 1998), 13.

64 Calvino, *Kybernetik und Gespenster*, 11.

65 Walter Benjamin, *Gesammelte Schriften. Unter der Mitwirkung von Theodor W. Adorno und Gershom Sholem herausgegeben von Rolf Tiedemann.* (Frankfurt am Main 1974), I, I, 71ff.

66 Cf. Betyna, *Kritik, Reflexion und Ironie*, 15.

67 Benjamin, *Gesammelte Schriften,* 86.

68 Walter Benjamin, *Selected Writings*, Volume 1: 1913–1926, ed. by Marcus Bullock and Michael W. Jennings (Harvard 1996), 164f.

premonition of creation is revealed when the form is transcended, and the writing process becomes visible. The postmodern protagonist, like Calvino's Palomar, is the seeker, interested in the plans of the world and invites the reader to participate in the search effort. The novel is the central medium of this complicity. In it, all participants reassure themselves of the possible ways of encountering the world.

Jacob Ølgaard Nyboe
(University of Iceland)

Let the Horses Sing and the Astral Lava Flow. On Homosexuality as Transcending Force in Bjørn Rasmussen's *Huden er det elastiske hylster der omgiver hele legemet* and Henrik Bjelke's *Saturn*

Abstract
The novels *Saturn* (Bjelke, 1974) and *Huden er det elastiske hylster der omgiver hele legemet* (Rasmussen, 2011) have nearly forty years between them, and both came out long after the historical romanticism. However, I shall demonstrate how they both are highly influenced by romantic ideas and share a yearning for re-enchantment through epiphany and a search for an outsider identity. In both texts, the rather bluntly depicted sexual activity between men allows for the main characters to transcend themselves and strive for a romantic experience of unification with something bigger. The urge to transgress boundaries is mirrored in compositional as well as stylistic features where openness, playfulness, and disregard for generic conventions rule. Yet, there are also differences in the extent to which the romantic projects of the protagonists are satisfactorily redeemed which will be shown in a comparison with universal romanticism and neoplatonic romanticism respectively.

Keywords
queer romanticism, transcendence, intertextuality, metaphysics of experience, epiphany

At first glance both *Huden er det elastiske hylster der omgiver hele legemet* [*The Skin is the Elastic Covering that Encases the Entire Body*] by Bjørn Rasmussen and Henrik Bjelke's *Saturn* [Saturn] may appear as typical postmodern novels due to their extensive mixing of registers and sampling of other texts. When looking closer, however, one discovers that rather than representing a postmodern levelling of values both texts are of an ideological, romantic nature.[1] Thus, the dissolving of stylistic and generic hierarchies serve to consolidate a hierarchy of a higher order in which a striving for self-transcendence and a connection to the *Weltgeist* is the ideal. The romanticism of the texts is strongly connected to a confession to the epiphanic and its potential for insight into a

1 For a discussion on postmodern value relativism (and some of its inherent contradictions) see Terry Eagleton, "The Contradictions of Postmodernism", *New Literary History 28*, no. 1 (Winter 1997): 1–6.

higher level of existence, and the epiphanic is itself again closely linked to the experience of male homosexuality, why it makes sense to talk of a queer romanticism. In the following I shall demonstrate how male on male sexuality by both Rasmussen and Bjelke is turned into an idealistic and spiritual practice that allows for the protagonists to transcend themselves. In other words, I shall argue that the novels, despite their explicit erotic content, are of a romantic rather than a pure pornographic nature. Along the way I will, through the work of philosopher Dorthe Jørgensen, discuss the romantic traits of the works in the light of the development of aesthetical perception throughout literary history.

Breathing that special air – Bjørn and the quest for transcendence

On the first page of *Huden* the narrator, Bjørn, recalls that at the age of twelve, all he dreamed of 'var at se op i en anden mands røvhul og trække et særligt vejr, jeg tænkte kærligheden, en fugls flaksen' [was looking up a man's asshole and breathing that special kind of air, I thought love, a fluttering bird].[2] We here learn that he, from childhood, has been longing for a different state of being through the altering of something as fundamental as the air he breathes. The Danish word *vejr* can denote *breath* (as in *trække vejret* [draw breath]) as well as *weather* thus making it ambiguous and potentially referring to both the inner and the outer world. Furthermore, it is obvious that the gateway to this altered state is perceived to be homosexual practice, in the quote metonymically and quite explicitly represented by the foreign asshole. But it is also linked to the concept of love as in a sequence a few pages later: 'siden han tog ridelæreren til roden i gin og gin… han har ikke trukket det særlige vejr, han kalder kærligheden, siden gin og gin' [since he took the riding instructor all the way to the hilt under gin and gin … he hasn't breathed that special air he calls love, not since gin and gin].[3] Thus, from the start an associative chain of transformation is formed: homosexuality – altered state – love.

As noted by Tobias Skiveren, Rasmussen's novel has been read through the lens of critical constructivist theory as well as a part of the materialistic turn with a focus on the body with all its material processes, needs, and restrictions.[4] Skiveren, however, proposes a third approach that, while respecting the former,

2 Bjørn Rasmussen, *Huden er det elastiske hylster der omgiver hele legemet* (København: Gyldendal, 2011), 5. Quotes in English are taken from the translation by Martin Aitken published by *Two Lines Press*, San Fransisco, 2019.

3 Rasmussen, *Huden*, 8.

4 Tobias Skiveren, "Ekstatisk nydelse i mere-end-menneskelige kroppe. Om tegn, affekt og kødets begær i Bjørn Rasmussens og Niels Henning Falk Jensbys debutromaner", *Edda 106*, no. 3 (2019): 181 f. https://doi.org/10.18261/issn.1500-1989-2019-03-02.

focuses more on an affect-oriented exploration of the bodily experiences of the narrator and the ecstatic pleasure connected with them. I intend to follow that path by further investigating the romantic and transcending nature of these experiences.[5]

Puns are abundant in the text, for instance in the form of anaphorical lists where the meaning of a word shifts and sometimes even changes lexical category. One example is a passage resembling a systematic poem where the same word is used as verbal imperative *stol* [trust] and substantive *stol* (chair) and through the use of ellipsis both meanings are present at once with the same word ending a sentence (chair) and beginning the next (trust).[6] As also noted by Skiveren, this is a reminder of one of the key insights of deconstructivism; the fundamental ambiguity of language.[7] But it is also part of a general endeavour to blur lines between borders, challenge categories and unify, here illustrated by the distinctions between word classes and between sentences being dissolved. On a compositional level, the demarcation between the text and the paratext is also annulled as the acknowledgements are integrated within the text itself.[8] In this passage we also learn that the author has 'hugget sætninger fra adskillige andre tekster' [been ripping off sentences from all over the place] thus also blurring the borders between the novel and the works of others (ranging from Marguerite Duras and Sylvia Plath to scientific works on anatomy and the sensory organs). Furthermore, the author and the narrator are being merged by letting the latter do the acknowledgements (the identity of the two was already hinted at by the coinciding names) leaving us in a space of uncertain borders between fiction and non-fiction (the testimony of lived experiences). The illustrations in the middle of the book (48–50) contribute to this effect. Here we see a boy with a horse, an evaluation sheet from a dressage tournament with Bjørn Rasmussen's name on it (along with the name of the horse Magna, also mentioned in the text) and a tree perfectly fitting a description made by the riding instructor on page 39. The intended effect of this is obvious; we must understand that the author did indeed attend horse shows and that the tree in the text is indeed referring to an actual tree in the extralinguistic reality. At the same time, the text is elsewhere obviously

5 Skiveren touches briefly upon the romantic aspect of the text in the following passage: 'Vi har at gøre med en art masochistisk revitalisering af den romantiske forestilling om at gå op i alnaturen' [We are dealing with a kind of masochistic revitalization of the romantic concept of being emerged into the all-encompassing nature]. Skiveren, "Ekstastisk nydelse", 190. My translation.

6 Rasmussen, *Huden*, 9.

7 Cf. Skiveren, "Ekstatisk nydelse", 183. The problem of the inherent ambiguity of language is probably most notably and clearly proposed in Paul de Man, "Semiology and Rhetoric", *Diacritics* 3, no. 3 (Autumn, 1979). https://doi.org/10.2307/464524.

8 Rasmussen, *Huden*, 90f.

fictionalized.[9] This is most obvious in several fairy tale inspired passages with magical elements where we follow the young Bjørn's development.[10] The text places its readers in an open zone of uncertainty and establishes a degree of performativity as described by Jon Helt Haarder's concept of *performative biographism.*[11] The integration of the fairy tale modus along with the aforementioned lists that resemble poetry point to a last significant formal feature of the text: The openness and neglect of common boundaries also apply to the use of genres that are mixed in a rather free manner. All in all, it is fair to say that the text both thematizes *and,* at the same time, enacts fluid boundaries and a form of radical openness.

On the thematical side, it is quite often borders between the body and its surroundings and/or the distinctions between traditional gender categories that are sought transgressed.[12] As a rather extreme example, we learn that the narrator has 'skåret et hul i mellemkødet lige under nosserne, fordi jeg gerne vil være en pige, jeg vil så gerne have en lille fisse, så jeg kan få pik i tre huller samtidig' [gouged a hole in my perineum just below my balls, because I want to be a girl, I want a little cunt of my own so I can get dicked in three holes at once].[13] It is worth noting that the fantasy of going beyond the given biological sex is combined with a dream of (an even higher degree of) penetration. This is also reflected in Bjørn's fantasy of drowning and letting the water (and everything else) run through him as well as the recurrent self-cutting.[14] The narrator's strong urge to transcend himself is never more present and closer to being fulfilled than in the relation to the riding instructor which is why the text can indeed be read as a love story.[15] The

9 For more on fictionality, see for instance Simona Zetterberg Gjerlevsen and Henrik Skov Nielsen, "Distinguishing Fictionality" in *Exploring Fictionality: Conceptions, Test Cases, Discussions*, ed. Cindie Aaen Maagaard et al (Odense: University Press of Southern Denmark, 2020), 19–39.

10 Rasmussen, *Huden*, 26–27 and 72–73. An example of magical elements is the talking horse on page 27.

11 Jon Helt Haarder, "Knausenstein's monster: Portraits of the author in a post-anthropocentric mirror", *Textual Practice 35*, no. 1 (2019), 73f. https://doi.org/10.1080/0950236X.2019.1655472.

12 The norm-critical potential and subversion of heteronormative gender systems has been discussed in several analyses, for instance Camilla Schwartz, "Take me to Neverland. Androgynitet, hysteri og voksenfobi i ny dansk litteratur", *EDDA 114*, no. 1 (2017): 24–24. https://doi.org/10.18261/issn.1500-1989-2017-01-03, and Iben Engelhardt Andersen og Mette-Marie Zacher Sørensen, "Krop, lov og ja! Fire noter om Bjørn Rasmussens roman *Huden er det elastiske hylster der omgiver hele legemet*", *Den blå port 91* (2012): 54–60.

13 Rasmussen, *Huden*, 86.

14 Rasmussen, *Huden*, 9, 11 and 16, 32, 61, 70. Often words are being cut into the skin, and as examined elsewhere there is an interesting relationship at play between writing practise, textual materiality and incarnation themes, cf. Lilian Munk Rösing: "Kød, blod og ord. Om nadveren som litterær topos", *Kultur og Klasse 123* (2017), 207f.

15 The urge for transcendence is also recognized by Eva Magelund Krarup as a key feature of

narrative might be fragmented but it clearly revolves around the strong desire towards the riding instructor and the immense effect he has on the narrator. This is the core of the text, which is also reflected in the recurrent scene that opens the two parts of the book, where the two lovers meet again at a later point in time and in which we learn that attraction is far from over.[16] In a sense, the whole book is written for the lover (cf. the first chapter title 'Elskeren' ['Loverman'], which is in the Danish version borrowed from Duras' *L'Amant*) whom Bjørn strives to be released from but at the same time neither can, nor will, let go of: 'Jeg skriver det her for at give slip på dig. Mit livs historie eksisterer ikke, men du gør, jeg gør…' [I'm a writing this so I can let go of you. My life story doesn't exist, but you do, I do…].[17]

The explanation for the narrator's fixation is to be found in the fulfilment of his transcendental yearning provided by the lover. The desire to 'look up a man's asshole and breathing that special kind of air' as stated on the very first page is, thus, being fulfilled by him: 'Jeg begraver næsen i revnen, fastgør læberne om det stramme kød, rosa og grå, og suger og slikker. Min tunge bryder gennem hans krans og kærtegner de indre vægge. / Jeg ser op gennem den sorte skakt. / Og hestene synger' [I bury my nose in the crack, fix my lips to the tight flesh, pink and gray, and proceed to suck and slubber and lick. My tongue penetrates the ring of his anus, caresses the inner walls. / I look up into the dark shaft. / And the horses sing].[18] The erotic encounter turns into a mystical experience symbolized by the singing horses as an echo of a typical motif in romanticism; the spiritual experience in which nature becomes spirited and filled with music.[19] The experience can be characterized as an epiphany in the joycean definition: 'a sudden spiritual manifestation'.[20] As demonstrated by Gísli Magnússon, the literary use

the work, and she too sees a connection to the self-cutting practice: 'Men cutteriet kan (også) læses som et forsøg på at overskride hudens grænse, så Bjørn kan træde i tættere kontakt med verdensmaterialiteten og den anden' [But the self-cutting can (also) be read as an attempt to transgress the borders of the skin, in order for Bjørn to come closer to the world-materiality and the other]. Eva Magelund Krarup, "(Ny)materielle fusioner", *Passage 77* (Summer 2017): 113–126. https://doi.org/10.7146/pas.v32i77.97043. My translation.

16 Rasmussen, *Huden*, 3 and 38.

17 Rasmussen, *Huden*, 85.

18 Rasmussen, *Huden*, 35.

19 Cf. for instance 'Skoven sang, og Havet sang og hans Hjerte sang med' [The forest sang, the sea sang, and the heart of the boy sang too] from the final scene of revelation in H. C. Andersens "Klokken" [The Bell] in *Eventyr med Illustrationer af Vilh. Pedersen* (København: C. A. Reitzel, 1850). Another example could be A. W. Schack von Staffeldts "Indvielsen" [Initiation] and the lines 'Da rundt en anden Natur der blev, / Vindene talte' [Then all around me the world was new: / The winds spoke] from *Digte 1804* (København: Universitetsboghandler Fr. Brummers Forlag, 1804),4. This is just to mention two of the most significant authors within Danish romanticism. My translation of Staffeldt and translation of Andersen by Jean Hersholt, The Hans Christian Andersen Centre (andersen.sdu.dk).

20 James Joyce, *Stephen Hero* (New York: New Directions, 1963), 211.

of epiphanies can be symptomatic of a romantic yearning for a re-enchanted world, here in the case of Knausgård: 'Just as the Romanticists, he yearns for a re-enchanted ("open") divine reality. The means of re-enchantment are peak experiences, epiphanies, and privileged moments experienced in nature, art, poetry, music, and love'.[21] The same can be said of Rasmussen with an emphasis on the carnal aspect of love. For Schlegel, nature is disenchanted when perceived as not the least mysterious and completely intelligible by reason.[22] This resonates in Weber's famous definition: 'there are no mysterious, incalculable forces that come into play, but… one can, in principle, master all things by calculation. This means that the world is disenchanted'.[23] I shall use the concept of disenchantment in this understanding and derived therefrom to describe the protagonists' experience of a world that is predictable, wonderless, and restricted in a way that leaves no room for the otherness they represent or the yearning they feel. Conversely, re-enchantment is the insistence on something *more* in the world that cannot be grasped by senses and pure reason alone. In the words of Schlegel, romantic poetry is re-enchanting because it 'points to what is higher, the infinite, [it offers] a hieroglyph of the… holy fullness of life of creative nature'.[24]

The singing of the horses is a recurrent trope, which is always connected with the riding instructor (with which the horses are obviously metonymically connected) and erotic ecstasy; when Bjørn is being penetrated deeply on page 53: 'Så sang hestene' [Then the horses sang], and when he is anticipating a new sexual encounter on page 81: 'Det skal ske igen / Hestene skal synge' [It's going to happen again / The horses are going to sing]. At one point, the narrator explicitly links the horse singing to a vision of spiritual oneness as he is imagining that the horses 'synger om natten. At det stålsatte hierarki opløses, og de bliver én fælles vilje, én varmblodig sang; flerstemmig, harmonisk, umærkelig' [sing in the night. I imagine the rigid hierarchy disintegrating and them becoming a single will, a single warm-blooded song; polyphonic, harmonious, imponderable].[25] It is this holistic vision that only the lover can redeem but always through a quite concrete and physical sexual encounter rather than a purely spiritual or psychological affinity. One can thus, with a term from Dorthe Jørgensen, talk about *metaphysics of experience* [*erfaringsmetafysik*] with a distinct sensory experi-

21 Gísli Magnússon, "The Aesthetics of Epiphany in Karl Ove Knausgård's *Min Kamp*", *Scandinavian Studies 92*, no. 3 (Fall 2020): 356.

22 Alison Stone, "Friedrich Schlegel, Romanticism, and the Re-enchantment of Nature", *Inquiry 48*, no. 1 (2005): 5. https://doi.org/10.1080/00201740510015338.

23 Max Weber, "Science as a Vocation" (1919), in *Essays in Sociology*, ed. H. H. Gerth and C. Wright Mills (New York: Routledge, 1948), 139.

24 Friedrich Schlegel, "Dialogue on poetry", trans. Ernst Behler and Roman Struc, in *German Romantic Criticism*, ed. A. Leslie Willson (New York: Continuum, 1982), 334.

25 Rasmussen, *Huden*, 60.

ence as basis for the spiritual epiphany.[26] The metaphysical and the physical experience are not opposites, but the former is inherent in the latter. The physical (in casu erotic) experience is what triggers the transcendence.[27] In alignment with this, Sharon Kim (through Edith Wharton) speaks of a 'modern epiphany which stresses the materiality of the aesthetic perception' and of epiphany as a material phenomenon in which the object is epiphanized, a process where 'the object, the experience becomes "spiritual"'.[28] This is why it makes sense when the narrator on page 47 describes himself as 'virkelig holistisk liderlig' [really holistically horny] and later, on the same page, makes a connection between romanticism and climaxing in a passage where the coherence of the text dissolves, mimicking the loss of control of the orgasm: 'ja / ja / det er romantik / det er det tætteste jeg kommer det er dig jeg elsker det er mig der elsker det er mig der er nej nu kommer jeg / nej nu kommer jeg nej nu nej / nu kommer jeg nu kommer jeg nej / nu nej nu nej / nej / nej' [yes / yes / this is romance / it's the closest I'll ever get / it's you I love it's me who's loving it's me who's oh no I'm coming now / oh no I'm coming now oh no now no / now no now no / no / no].[29] The novel circles around the loved one but only because he grants access to the desired borderless state of unity. It therefore becomes hard to tell whether the riding instructor constitutes a transcending force because Bjørn loves him, or whether Bjørn loves him because of this transcending force. On a linguistic level, the declaration of love and the orgasm is also being closely linked in the passage above as well as in the following: 'Så knappede han sine bukser op, hev sin store brune pik frem og pissede mig på brystet, i håret, i munden. / Jeg kom. Jeg skreg. Jeg elsker ham' [The he unbuttoned his trousers, got his own big brown cock out, and pissed all over my chest, in my hair, my mouth / I came. I screamed. I love him].[30]

The above quoted passage is one amongst many where the depicted sexual activity is of a sadomasochistic nature, and this seems to be connected to the general project of breaking down boundaries. It is significant that we are not just dealing with a love story but with a *queer* such, which is engaged in exploring taboos and challenging norms. This corresponds with the so-called *affective revolution* of the historical romanticism which 'nurtured a promiscuous pro-

26 Cf. for instance Dorthe Jørgensen: *Skønhedens metamorfose. De æstetiske idéers historie* (Odense: Syddansk Universitetsforlag, 2001), 371f and 394f.

27 It is thus no coincidence that the only time Krarup mentions romanticism in relation to the text (to my knowledge as the only one besides Skiveren) it is in connection to materiality. Krarup, "(Ny)materielle", 122.

28 Sharon Kim: "Edith Wharton and Epiphany", *Journal of Modern Literature 29*, no. 3 (Spring 2006): 150–151. https://doi.org/10.1353/jml.2006.0030.

29 Rasmussen, *Huden*, 47. The slashes are part of the text adding to the feeling of fragmentation. The Danish word *romantik* translates into romanticism as well as romance.

30 Rasmussen, *Huden*, 22.

liferation of sexualities, gender identities, and forms of intimacy'.[31] This, sometimes forgotten, revolutionary side to romanticism is also being re-actualized by the book, as Bjørn pushes back and often times rages against the norms in his struggle to find a place in a highly norm regulated world into which he does not fit easily as we, for instance, see in the following: 'Da Bjørn var voksen kunne han ikke længere tale. Da han var født ind i en mandlig verden, en kvindelig verden, havde han ikke sit eget sprog' [When Bjørn became a grown-up he could no longer speak. Born into a masculine world, a feminine world, he had no language of his own].[32] The sexual excesses and the self-harm are intertwined with a harsh critique of a binary gender system that he feels alienated from and repulsed by.[33] This repressing system seems to be particularly strong in the small hometown of the narrator on the West Coast of the Danish mainland. Hence, Bjørn's rage, in several cases, takes the form of highly sarcastic descriptions of this town (as a representative of general patterns, of course). A passage revolving around a pun on the city name Lemvig (*lem* can also mean dick, *vig* also means yield) provides a humorous, yet harsh, critique of heteronormativity where it is presented as mandatory to harass bypassing women if you are a man (with a *lem*).[34] This harassment culture is furthermore being linked with Christianity in its exposure of the hypocritic behaviour of 'good Christians' and *slut-shaming* as men are obliged to force their sexuality on women whereas the woman in turn 'grows removed from God' if she gives into the pressure.[35] In this disenchanted and unpleasant environment, where even the religious is clearly profaned, the narrator's attempt to re-enchant through homosexual ecstasy can be viewed as both an escape and a rebellion. The obvious norm-critique is directed outwards towards social and institutional oppression, but it is always also – and foremost I claim – connected with Bjørn's romantic yearning for something more: a path to insight and higher states of experience. Accordingly, the text ends with a highly energetic and ecstatic future-vision (year 2060) of the two lovers being united and in turn dissolved into the light. I here quote only the last part of the fully capitalized scream-like passage which also repeats key motifs from the text such as the

31 Adriana Craciun: "Romantic poetry, sexuality, gender" in *The Cambridge Companion to British Romantic Poetry*, ed. James Chandler and Maureen N. McLane (Cambridge: Cambridge University Press, 2008), 157.

32 Rasmussen, *Huden*, 74.

33 Although there are also momentary glimpses of a wish to be able to fit into it, i. e., when he, in turn, wishes that he himself or the lover had a vagina (*Huden*, Rasmussen, 86 and 45). For a discussion of this ambiguity see Felix Thorsen Katzenelson et al: *Det er en krop der taler* (Roskilde: Roskilde Universitetscenter, 2017), 37–39.

34 Rasmussen, *Huden,* 41.

35 The city of Lemvig is known to be a Christian stronghold with a museum for religious art and large branches of the two conservative Christian sects Home Missions and Jehovah's Witnesses.

singing horses and the looking up into the dark shaft of an asshole: 'VI ER DET POETISKE INVENTAR I DET HER KØKKEN, DER SØNDERDELES I LYS OG REGENERERER I MØRKE SOM ROLIGHED OG INGEN MODSTAND OG [WE ARE THE POETIC PARAPHERNALIA OF THIS KITCHEN, BROKEN UP IN LIGHT AND REGENERATED IN DARKNESS, TRANQUILITY ITSELF AND NO RESISTANCE AND].[36] From the first to the last page, a yearning for self-transcendence is paramount, and it is unfolded in correspondence with the category-defying radical openness of the text quite illustratively reflected in the very last word being 'AND' with no punctuation mark. By refusing to close the sentence, the text insistingly stays open – as the future to which the ending is referring. Magnússon claims that 'the category of "the open" designates one of the ways in which the Romantic strategy of the re-enchantment is carried into the twentieth-century modernism', and this seems to also hold true in the case at hand.[37] In the quote above, *the open* is an existential category, borrowed from Rilke, which is highly relevant for the freedom seeking protagonist and which, in the novel, is also being supplemented by formal features of openness.

Enkidu and the erotic awakening

Henrik Bjelke's *Saturn* states even more explicit claims about the liberating potential of homosexuality (and non-normative behaviour as such) as well as male on male sexual practice as a path to mystical, epiphanic experiences and enlightenment The main character (mostly, but not always, the narrator) is developing his own spiritual theory, strongly influenced by Hinduism and Buddhism, in which his sexual discoveries play a key role. On a formal level, the novel is at least as experimental and fragmented as that of Rasmussen with its own boundary-defying and open nature: it jumps in time and place without warning; it shifts language on a regular basis and include longer passages in French, Italian, and English; it provides forty pages of footnotes with word explanations and references; it mixes a long range of stylistic registers including a *novel within the novel* and stream of consciousness with abrupt and unfinished sentences; and finally it makes a great amount of intertextual references, most notably – but definitely not restricted – to the Mesopotamian *Epic of Gilgamesh*, as will be demonstrated.[38]

36 Rasmussen, *Huden*, 93.

37 Magnússon, "The Aesthetics", 355.

38 In addition, the text is a highly self-reflective work of metaliterature discussing its own premises and the premises for literature as such both within the text itself and in the interplay with the footnotes and the mottos. Thus, it is questionable where the paratext ends and the text begins, also here the different levels seem intertwined or the borders between them simply

In short, it is a highly learned, ambitious, and challenging novel of an encyclopaedic nature, and it is also generally acknowledged as such by critics.[39] Within this fairly complex structure, we follow a writer who is living with his wife and son in Menton, France, where he has affairs with an Italian woman followed by a young American man whom he later (without luck) pursues in a series of travels during which he engages in several homosexual encounters. Finally, we find him relatively harmonic and happy reunited with his wife, so merged into the many digressions and excesses there is the structure of a classical *bildungsroman.* A turning point is when a director, Rod Steiger, who is weirdly enough also the personal doctor of the protagonist, decides to shoot a film based on Gilgamesh in Menton.[40] This becomes the catalyst of the narrator's introduction to his male lover as well as an increased mixing of different narrative levels, as the relation between the two men is mirrored in that of Gilgamesh and Enkidu from the epic to a degree where their names are being transferred to our characters. The first erotic encounter, a key scene for the novel in general – and for my discussion in particular – follows one of the many direct quotes from the Gilgamesh epic and a page long anaphorical poem where a lyrical subject is envisioning a connection between his own bodily fluids and an existential plane: 'Mit verdensbillede skal drukne i min sperma og i mit blod og min sperma og mit blod skal igen forsvinde i mit verdensbillede' [My worldview shall drown in my sperm and in my blood and my sperm and my blood, in return, shall vanish in my worldview].[41] Quite characteristically, there is no intermediating bridge between the two highly unalike texts, and they can be seen as respectively mythological and thematical introductions to the sex scene that follows, again without any explicit linguistic bridging and without any prior background for the meeting. We are, so to speak, placed *in medium coitum.* Only later, we learn that the sexual partner is a young American who plays the role of Enkidu in the film and is consequently referred to by this name by the narrator. The intercourse is described in detail over three pages and noteworthy is the emphasis on self-transcendence in a highly en-

defied. Cf. Jesper Hede, *Note til Saturns ødemark. Bjelkes* Saturn *og Eliots* Wasteland (Aarhus: Aarhus Universitet, 2007), 4f.

39 See, for instance, Jimmi Michelsen, "Bestemt ikke læsernes kæledægge", *Synsvinkler 11,* no. 27 (2002): 94–103 and René Rasmussen, *Bjelke lige i øjet* (København: Forlaget Politisk Revy, 2000), 165f.

40 The use of the same name for different characters, or perhaps rather the merging of them into one, is one of many ways in which the comprehension of the work gets disturbed. For an overview over the character names and the relations see Hede, *Note*, 3. This technique can, of course, be viewed as a way of turning the characters into a kind of archetypes by letting the names cover more general qualities rather than specific personalities. A reading that is supported by the fact that a lot of the names are taken from the ancient epic; Dr. Steiger is for example also referred to as Dr. Shamash (the Mesopotamian sun god).

41 Henrik Bjelke, *Saturn* (København: Arena, 1974), 192. All translations from this book are my own.

ergetic, hyperintense prose with elements of cosmic imagery. The rhythmical penetration is hammering intense energy into the narrator with the following effect: 'Denne psykisk tilfredsstillende vanartethed konkretiseres strengt og uigendriveligt og jeg bliver mere og mere fri. Fri til uanede dybder i mig selv, adgang til uanede spejle i selvets refleksvægge' [This psychologically satisfying abnormality is sternly and irrefutably concretized and I become freer and freer. Free to unimaginable depths within myself, access to unimaginable mirrors in the reflective walls of the self].[42] We see here both the intense feeling of self-knowledge emerging from the sexual act as well as the importance of the norm-defying character of it (the abnormality). The narrator is being liberated by penetration which is being linked to a mystical epiphanic experience of expanding the boundaries of the self: 'Jeg er titusinder, jeg er alle andre, jeg er alle … det tredje øje, jeg er transcendens … brudt ud af den eneste mulige frihedens vej: forkertheden, jeg er underkastet nye love i tid og rum' [I am tens of thousands, I am everyone else, I am everyone … the third eye, I am transcendence … I have broken out by the only possible way to freedom: inappropriateness, I am submitted to new laws in time and space].[43] The dissolving of the self to become part of a greater whole is a well-established spiritual state and the text itself makes explicit references to traditional mysticism in the form of transcendence and the third eye, known from Hinduism where it is connected with states of higher insight, enlightenment, and out-of-body-experiences.[44] The very physical sexual experience forms the basis of a mystical transcendence and once again the concept of metaphysics of experience seems highly relevant. As climax is approaching, a cosmological dimension is added as his penis awakens and feels 'ikke sperma – men astral lava spile de undersøiske kabler op og nærme sig med billioner af kilometers hastighed i sekundet' [not sperm – but astral lava dilate the underwater cables and approach with trillions of kilometres speed per second].[45] The scale of the ecstasy is presented as extra-earthly, of astronomical dimensions, and extreme energy. Finally, leading up to a synchronized explosion, the boundary of the self is dissolved once again as the penetrator and the penetrated becomes one: 'Alle dele af min underkrop er i aktivitet, jeg knepper mig selv, jeg er ham, der knepper mig, det er et, han og jeg er et rødglødende, rytmisk hele. Eksplosionen sker på samme tid.' [All parts of my lower body are activated, I am fucking myself, I am he, who is fucking me, it is one, he and I are one red hot,

42 Bjelke, *Saturn*, 193.
43 Bjelke, *Saturn*, 194.
44 See, for instance, Lawrence A. Babb, "Glancing: Visual Interaction in Hinduism", *Journal of Anthropological Research 37*, no. 4 (Winter 1981): 387–401. https://doi.org/10.1086/jar.37.4.3629835.
45 Bjelke, *Saturn*, 194.

rhythmic whole. The explosion is simultaneous].[46] The homo-prefix of homosexuality is symbolically being extended to the identity of the acting parts; no distinction between them is made, they are homomorph to a degree where they become one. Here, we see another reason, in addition to the anti-normativity, why it is homosexuality specifically and not just sexuality in general that holds a self-expanding potential for the narrator, namely this mirror effect.[47]

The enlightening potential of homosexuality is being theorized upon in several places in the text, and one can almost talk about a spiritual-sexual manifesto made up from interrelated fragments (due to the generally fragmented style). For instance, even before the encounter, physical love between men is being directly linked with the potential of a higher insight of universal character, with a romantic idea of an all-encompassing universal love.[48] The young American lover initiates our narrator to this form of love and turns his theoretical speculations into practice but also adds his own reflections to the philosophical system: 'Enkidu talte til mig om omvendtheden som middel til komplettering af verdensbilledet ... Om skønheden og naturligheden ved at manden kærtegner manden i stedet for at tilintetgøre ham ... Om omkalfatring af instinkterne og afkastning af survivalnormtyranniet. Om herliggørelse ved "underkastelsen"' [Enkidu spoke to me of inversion as a means to complete the world view ... Of the beauty and naturalness in man caressing man instead of destroying him ... Of the radical change of instincts and rejection of the survival norm tyranny. Of the glorification by "submission"].[49] It is clear how the idea of queer sexuality as a path to a more balanced perspective and a way of obtaining harmony instead of destruction is being supported here; as well as the rebellion against norms as also presented earlier. The education the narrator receives is in other words ideological as well as physical, and the two levels are deeply interconnected. Noteworthy is the view on submission as something glorifying, and it seems to be a point in both novels that liberation and self-forgetfulness relates to submitting oneself to the other and letting oneself be penetrated, and the protagonists both insistingly take the position of the penetrated rather than the penetrator.[50]

In the ancient epic Enkidu is a *wild man* who is matching Gilgamesh in strength but also forming an antithesis by being connected with the natural world as

46 Bjelke, *Saturn*, 194f.

47 The affair with the Italian Claudia never leads to a similar level of transcendence or mystical insight. The liberating potential of the merging with another is hinted at in one of their sexual encounters but remains unfulfilled. Cf. Bjelke, *Saturn*, 91.

48 Cf. Bjelke, *Saturn*, 138, where it is described how men should discover each other as sexual partners and through that discover themselves, the universe, and universal love.

49 Bjelke, *Saturn*, 226. This is but a short excerpt from a more than two pages long speech by Enkidu in which he almost takes the role of a preacher.

50 For Bjørn, there is a single exception from the rule, being explicitly singled out as an exception. Cf. Rasmussen, *Huden,* 46 and Bjelke, *Saturn*, 268.

opposed to the cultured and civilized Gilgamesh. It is this function of complementing and completing Gilgamesh that is mirrored in the relationship between the American and the narrator. The death of Enkidu in the epic sends the grieving Gilgamesh on a quest for eternal life in the shape of *the flower of immortality* and, parallelly, our narrator is heartbroken when his personal Enkidu disappears after the filming, and he sets out on his own quest to search for him.[51] Both missions are unsuccessful at first glance but force the two heroes to accept death and loss as part of life and thus contribute to their personal growth and the completeness of their character. Noteworthily, the narrator also experiences that the initiation and physical-spiritual insight that was brought forth by the meeting with the American is not restricted to him. Through a wide range of sexual encounters, he realizes that the mind-expanding metaphysics of experience can be obtained with other partners. This makes the original male lover a representation of, and an initiation to, a more general principle which can be accessed through other paths, in opposition to Rasmussen's novel where the riding instructor remains the focus of Bjørn's longing and dreams of transcendence. This explains why the American is being coupled with the mythological figure of Enkidu, lending him a more timeless and universal aura and why the narrator keeps recognizing him in strangers on the streets during his travels; Enkidu is (potentially) every man.[52] The journey, thus, becomes a continuation and expansion of his newfound sexual capacity and the spiritual growth that lies within it:

> 'Alle mænd er omvandrende banker for denne energi og jeg selv er enormt rig og bliver stedse rigere. Jeg ejer alle og ingen. Ingen ejes af mig og jeg ejes af ingen. … Just derfor er fallisk-anal aktivitet mellem mænd den rigeste form for drift fordi den medfører den største oplevelse af uventet frihed. … År for år livet igennem er denne mulighed tilstede. Thi verden er fuld af utålmodige unge mænd, der alle er lige rige og lige tørstige efter deres adgang til jégtabs-planet' [All men are wandering banks of this energy and I myself am immensely rich and keep getting richer. I own everyone and no one. No one is owned by me, and I am owned by no one. … For exactly this reason is anal-phallic activity among men the richest form of urge because it provides the biggest experience of unexpected freedom. … Year for year through life this opportunity is present. For the world is full of impatient young men who all are equally rich and equally thirsty for their access to the plane of self-loss].[53]

He discovers homosexuality as a general meditation practice and direct access to *the plane of self-loss* and realizes that the spirituality and release of energy lies as a potential in each anal-phallic encounter, which leads to the many sexual encounters during his travels.[54] Here, it becomes clear how his world has been re-

51 Bjelke, *Saturn*, 240f.
52 Cf. Bjelke, *Saturn,* 258 and 281.
53 Bjelke, *Saturn*, 222–224.
54 Erik Svendsen reads the novel as an *explicit gay story* ('eksplicit bøssehistorie') and is sur-

enchanted, with a deeper dimension of existence potentially available to him on every corner. Before the initiation, he is presented as disillusioned and joyless with no real engagement in his surroundings, and even literature that, for an author, should provide an outlet, an access to deeper insight is described as a disease that only brings him frustration.[55] So in a sense the erotic awakening can also be seen as a source of renewed artistic joy and energy.

The development of the narrator in turn leads to a state of spiritual maturity with which he returns to his family. It remains an open question whether he is really done exploring the new side of his sexuality: 'Vil jeg behøve fyre på samme måde hele vejen igennem siden jeg opdagede betydningen af Enkidu?' [Will I need guys in the same way perpetually since I discovered the meaning of Enkidu?].[56] But, in any case, he is altered from his experiences, and in the following passage it is implied that his need for outer stimuli in general has been reduced, due to a new level of insight: 'Men følelsen af tomhed i mig ... er afløst af en extase ved selve tomheden: den er ikke tom' [But the feeling of emptiness within me ... has been substituted by an ecstasy from emptiness itself: it is not empty].[57] Once again, the re-enchantment theme is present as a feeling of emptiness which has been replaced by a sense of gratifying fulfilment. Ecstasy has, through his spiritual journey, become something he can produce from within himself, from a meditation on emptiness, and thus it no longer necessarily has to come from the other (that was all along represented as a mirror of himself). This somehow corresponds with Edith Wharton's view on the epiphanic in the bildungsroman where epiphany, however intense, is not a goal in itself but rather constitutes an important catalyst for the growth of the protagonist as 'a flash of insight can be

prised, as am I, by how little this is recognized in other readings. He is also rather critical of its glorification of male homosexuality and even sees in it a latent misogyny, cf. Erik Svendsen, "Maksimum af 'sædmængde' og maksimum af bøssefrisættelse i *Saturn*", in *Sytten postkort til Henrik Bjelke*, ed. Anders Juhl Rasmussen og Tue Kjerstein Kristensen (Hellerup: Forlaget Spring, 2005), 71–85. I agree that the celebration of male on male sexuality and almost ceremonial appraisal of male relationships can seem quite exclusive within a gender-equality context. It certainly assigns the male partaker in homosexual activities the same position as that of the genius artist in the historical romanticism, with a special sensibility and a privileged access to the higher levels of existence (which follows directly from the main argument of my article). Instead of focusing on the inherent inappropriateness in this (which can indeed be derived), I choose to see the text as a testimony of a particular and personal journey of enlightenment in which homosexuality plays a key role. It does not per se exclude other paths, even though the text can come out a bit bombastic and ideological at times. The glorification of *a man's world* is elsewhere being counterweighted by a celebration of a female principle (freed form the hierarchies and violence of masculinity), e. g.: Bjelke, *Saturn*, 175. See also René Rasmussen's discussion of gender relations in Rasmussen, *Bjelke*, 191–197.

55 See for instance Bjelke, *Saturn, 118* and Rasmussen, *Bjelke*, 182–188.

56 Bjelke, *Saturn*, 300.

57 Ibid.

only a beginning'.[58] Since being released from the profane world through the epiphanic transcendence, our narrator has now returned to it, but in and altered and wiser state.

Postcoitus – closing remarks and reflections

The epiphany as discussed in my analysis is closely related to what Dorthe Jørgensen defines as the aesthetic itself. What makes the aesthetic aesthetic and the sublime sublime is an element of transcendence, at one and the same time present and ungraspable, pointing to a "more" in the world that we sense but find it hard to clearly verbalize.[59] This is related to the religious and can be described as an experience of the divine but, in opposition to the religious that is based in pure perception, the aesthetic is always based in a concrete sensual experience (and is thus not directed towards any specific divinity).[60] This is why Jørgensen talks about a metaphysics of experience and also why we can meet the aesthetic outside of art, for instance in an overwhelming landscape – or in carnal union with another person. However, art and literature are privileged places for evoking the aesthetic with their ability to create spaces freed from worldly speculations on purpose and utility. It is thus a tradition of insisting on the truly aesthetic, which was particularly emphasized in romanticism, into which the novels inscribe themselves. Rather than just describing the state of transcendence, they also seek to evoke an aesthetic moment, in a sense merging theme and ambition of the text, which explains the distinct style and high degree of form awareness. As Jørgensen points out, romanticism is not foremost a specific style but rather a way of perceiving the world and performing as an artist, it represents a certain atmosphere through which the world is interpreted.[61] This is a reason why the romantic can persist through time in different stylistic transformations – even for texts which also display ugliness, brutality, and a disturbing form as the novels at hand. As an example, Jørgensen highlights Baudelaire with his attempt to find beauty within the hideous in a compact form with intense expressiveness.[62] She even regards him as normative for the so-called *romantic-modern* with his duality between divinity and spleen, a combination that is indeed also present in both *Huden* and *Saturn.* The novels are, of course, not plainly works of romanticism or even purely romantic-modern. They

58 Kim, "Edith Wharton", 168.

59 Dorthe Jørgensen: *Aglaias dans. På vej mod en æstetisk tænkning*, (Aarhus: Aarhus Universitetsforlag, 2008), 61.

60 Jørgensen, *Aglaias*, 62.

61 Jørgensen, *Skønhedens*, 279.

62 Jørgensen, *Skønhedens*, 307.

are complex works of their own time incorporating different sources of inspiration; in the case of Bjelke, for instance, the sexual liberation project and newfound interest in psychoanalysis and eastern mysticism of the hippie generation; and for Rasmussen *the material turn*, contemporary queer- and gender theories as well as, of course, the authors he "steals" from in his work. But, at the core, they both pursue a goal that is romantic in nature which is why it makes sense to hold them up against two original romantic positions, as I will now do for the remainder of this article. The point is to demonstrate how they, all their similarities aside, display significant differences when it comes to the degree of redemption of their respective romantic yearnings.

For Bjørn, all the romantic longing is centred around the riding instructor and the sadomasochistic relationship of which he is unable to let go. In small glimpses of ecstasy, he comes close to a mystic revelation of self-expansion, but a full and long-lasting satisfaction cannot be obtained as it is too bound up on an impossible relationship and fleeting moments of (extreme) sex.[63] This is why the book must end in a vision of the future in which the riding instructor is also present and where they both are dissolved. A lasting satisfaction or inner peace can only be achieved by the final annihilation of the self, which explains why fantasies of death are recurrent throughout the book – in Bjørn's desire to drown, as mentioned before, but also in a repeated wish to explode in the mud in a trench next to the lover.[64] Several times he attempts to conform to norms (to some degree) and lead a *regular* life with a job.[65] These attempts are, however, futile, and the *wholesome* normalized life is being directly sneered at; for instance, when he has taken a job as a personal assistant for a middle class lady and lists up all his *normal* activities in an accumulative, sarcastic style: 'Bjørn køber en lampe, en radio, et tv, en computer og et abonnement på en avis. ... Bjørn siger 1000 mange tak for de søde hilsner. ... Bjørn er klar, parat, rede til at blive voksen. ... Så fik havemøblerne olie, det ku' de godt lide. Så er den weekend overstået øv øv' [Bjørn buys a lamp, a radio, a TV, a computer, and a newspaper subscription. ... Bjørn says thanks a zillion for all your lovely messages. ... Bjørn is ready, set,

63 The riding instructor thus, may be viewed as representing *little a* in the terminology of Jacques Lacan; the object for a desire which is always elusive and unattainable (jf. Jacques Lacan: *The Seminar of Jacques Lacan. Book VI: Desire and it's Interpretation* (Dublin: Lacan in Ireland, Cormac McCallagher, 2011), 227f). Indeed, a more psychoanalytical inspired approach to the text would be meaningful, and a such would look more into the highly intricate and semi-incestuous relationship to the mother which I have intentionally left out here as it falls beyond the scope of the article.

64 Cf. Rasmussen, *Huden*, 42 and 66.

65 At one point he works as a prostitute which can be said to be on the fringe of society, but for Bjørn it is still a way of fitting into a structure and building up an everyday life. He is extremely good at the job (jf. Rasmussen, *Huden*, 31) but performs it without any passion and ends up leaving when the riding instructor orders him to refrain from sex for a year.

raring to be an adult. … So, that's the garden furniture treated for the season, look how the wood just loves it. Another weekend gone before you know it].[66] The irony is easily derived from the hidden quotation of clichéd languages as well as the inherent social and consumerist clichés (and the tiresome, long list of banalities in itself), making it obvious that Bjørn is only playing a well-adjusted adult by saying and doing what one is supposed to do. The feeling of disenchantment is strong here, with life being presented as something completely predictable and scripted, as well as in a later passage ridiculing the idea of a wholesome and gender-stable *I:* 'Det dygtige jeg, det købedygtige jeg, det købte jeg. Det inficerede, det IKEA-ficerede, det producerede, det laminerede jeg. Det kønnede, det kernede, det kernesunde jeg.' [The competent individual, the individual with purchasing power. The purchased individual: The infected, IKEA-lized, fabricated, laminated individual. The gendered, gentrified, bright-eyed, rosy-cheeked individual].[67] The gendered and norm-adjusted *healthy* individual is presented as infected and deeply intertwined with consumerism and standardization, satirically represented by the neologism 'IKEA-lized'. He clearly cannot adjust to this form of life which is the direct opposite of his romantic yearning for re-enchantment. The position of Bjørn can thus be compared to that of the romanticists who subscribed to neoplatonism. In Denmark, this direction is most notably represented by Staffeldt who, following an initiation to a higher sphere and a sense of unitedness with the world spirit, concludes his most famous poem as follows: 'Dog blev fra nu for Tanke og Trang / Jorden et Fængsel; / Vel lindrer ved Anelse, Drøm og Sang / Hiertet sin Længsel, / Dog brænder mig Kysset jeg kiender ei Fred / Førend jeg drager Himlene ned!' [Yet, since then each thought and desire / became imprisoned by earth / Though intuition, dreaming, and singing / Ease the heart's longing / The kiss keeps burning, I know of no peace / Until I bring the heavens down to earth].[68] As in the poem, Bjørn's momentary glimpses of a higher state of being is followed by the realization that it can never be maintained as long as he is bound by the conforming structures of worldly existence. As a result, he is being torn between the knowledge of a higher state of existence and the impossibility of obtaining it permanently while bound by the profanity of earthly life. That is the true suffering of a neoplatonic romanticist.

In comparison, the position of Bjelke's narrator is rather that of *universal romanticism* and therefore a more positive and satisfying one. He manages to integrate the revelations of his own initiation into his daily life thus avoiding the torment of being torn between spheres. Throughout the book, his development can be compared to that of the apostle Simon Peter in a poem by the most

66 Rasmussen, *Huden*, 75–76.
67 Rasmussen, *Huden*, 30.
68 Staffeldt, "Indvielsen", 4. My translation.

prominent Danish universal romanticist, Adam Oehlenschläger. His revelation is condensed as follows at the end of the text, after a long description of his initiation to nature and Jesus (which are completely intertwined in the understanding of the poem): 'Saae du, da den tykke Taage fra dit kiekke Øie faldt, / At for sig er Alting Intet, men i Alt er Alting Alt?' [As the dim fog fell from your bright eye, did you see / That separated all is nothing, but in wholeness everything is all].[69] As the apostle in Oehlenschläger's reinterpretation, the narrator discovers a fundamental connectedness in the world; instead of mourning that one is not able to bring the higher sphere down to earth, it becomes a matter of realizing that it is already here. Accordingly, in the end we meet a person rather harmonically reunited with his family and ready to commit himself to them and, more significantly, to life itself, which is now perceived as a miracle. Here he is talking directly to his wife: '[Jeg] så dig, adlød makrokosmiske opfordringer til at *ville* leve og formåede ganske umagisk, det jeg formår. Og en by og et hav bød mig ind til sig og ned i sig og mit væsen strømmede dybt ned og helt ind i en hellig befrugtnings mikrokosmiske indigo … Miracolo' [[I] saw you, obeyed macrocosmical instigations to *want* to live and managed, quite unmagically, to do what I am able to. And a city and an ocean invited me into and down under them and my true self floated deep down and all the way into the microcosmical indigo of a holy fertilization … Miracolo].[70] It is clear how his cosmological experiences and insights are integrated into his everyday life with which he is now connected and in flow. To underline this, the final scene depicts a feeling of a higher unity and fundamental acceptance during an activity as profane as defecation:

> 'I sådanne øjeblikke af enhed, virkelig samhørsfølelse mellem det menneskeliges mineralske, vegetabilske og zoologiske identiteter, forstår man også, at man har været akkurat stærk nok til at tåle forceringen mellem ufødthed og fødsel, mellem ikke-tilstedeværelse og tilstedeværelse, mellem "død" og "liv"' [In such moments of unity, true feeling of coexistence between mineral, vegetable, and zoological identities of the human, one realizes that one has been precisely strong enough to overcome the hedge between being unborn and birth, between non-existence and existence, between "death" and "life"].[71]

That an everyday act like going to the toilet can bring forth such an invigorating feeling of connectedness and balance is exemplificatory for the development of the narrator. Admittedly, the scene also allows for a more satirical reading by being a bit too much, and the ending as such can seem a little too neat and well-

69 Adam Oehlenschäger: *Poetiske skrifter* (København: J. H. Schubothe, 1805), 457. My translation.

70 Bjelke, *Saturn*, 307.

71 Bjelke, *Saturn*, 307–308.

rounded considering the chaotic wildness displayed throughout the book.[72] However, if we read the text at face value (and even if we were to omit the reunion in the end) this is the story of a positive spiritual growth. By seeing beyond the immediate physical world, he becomes able to return to it in a higher state of enlightenment. Dorthe Jørgensen reflects on the epiphanic experience, that one can be mesmerized by the pleasure of the transcendence experience and seek its repetition by the shortest path. Or one can make the realization of the "more" of the transcendence subject to philosophical or artistic scrutiny – thereby ensuring that a possible repetition occurs on a higher level.[73]

In both novels the protagonists set out on the shortest path to a repetition of the epiphanic ecstasy; in Bjørn's case by repeatedly circling back to the riding instructor and for Bjelke's nameless narrator by engaging with the abundant stream of willing young men. Only in the latter case is this pattern broken by a philosophical transformation to a higher form of insight. But at a metalevel both texts are artistic explorations and expansions of the epiphanic experience, offering their readers the chance to co-experience its re-enchanting aura as well as to reflect upon its nature. Despite their differences and varying levels of redemption or optimism, the narrators both represent an intense insistence on self-expansion and the transgression of social and psychological boundaries. Queer sexuality is paramount in this pursuit as part of a general rebellion against restrictive norms but foremost as a liberating and transcending force that gives access to another level of existence where the horses sing, and

---

72 The ending is somewhat controversial. One critic called it fabricated ('postuleret'), Torben Brostrøm, "Et syndflodssagn som ender alt for godt", in *Ti års kritik*, ed. Torben Brostrøm (København: Gyldendal, 1975) and another finds it even *shrilly* fabricated, held up against the highly appraised gay dream unfolding right up to it, Svendsen, "Maksimum", 77. While I do see how this impression could arise, I still think they tend to neglect the quite obvious psychological-spiritual development of the character as well as the general playfulness and openness of the work. If the whole work plays with our expectations and makes it difficult to maintain an unambiguous understanding, an ending that has us wondering about its own authenticity seems to be in full alignment with rather than in contrast to the preceding text (and as shown in an earlier quote, the narrator explicitly keeps it an open question whether his homoerotic adventures are fully behind him). Rasmussen ("*Bjelke*", 214) perceives the ending as ironic and diagnoses the narrator as 'fastholdt i en anal tilstand … cementeret i en sproglig galskab, der hverken giver ham et sted at være eller helt tilintetgør ham' [kept in an anal state … cemented in a linguistic madness that neither gives him a place to be nor destroys him completely]. This is in accordance with his general analysis of the text as *diseased language* and the narrator as mentally ill into which the ending in an unironic version would not fit. Even though the text provides some support for this reading, I find it unnecessarily negative and narrow, considering the epiphanic ecstasy, the energy, and the overall playfulness of the text, as I have tried to demonstrate. In doing so, I might have become guilty of downplaying some of the more pessimistic passages, but the fact that the text can be read in quite different ways is also a mere testimony to its complexity – on which we can all agree.

73 Cf. Dorthe Jørgensen, *Viden og visdom. Spørgsmålet om de intellektuelle* (Frederiksberg: Det lille forlag, 2002), 87.

the astral lava flows freely. Both novels, thus, are of a queer romantic nature and constitute strong, highly aestheticized defences for openness and otherness.

About the Authors

Kasper Lægring is a New Carlsberg Foundation Postdoctoral Fellow in Art History at Aarhus University. He recently organized the large exhibition *The Joy of Everyday Life – in the Netherlands and Denmark* at the Nivaagaard Collection (2024). He serves on the Editorial Board of the journal *MDCCC 1800*, published by Venice University Press, and is an Associate Member of CODART, the international network for curators of Dutch and Flemish art. His current research explores the impact of emotions on art, with a particular focus on genre painting. Kasper is also the Second Vice President of the European Architectural History Network (EAHN) for the term 2024–2026, serving alongside Panagiotis Farantatos.

School of Communication and Culture – Art History
Aarhus University
kl@cc.au.dk

Anna Bohlin is a Professor of Nordic Literature at the University of Bergen, Norway. Recent publications include the cross-disciplinary anthologies *Tracing the Jerusalem Code III. The Promised Land: Christian Cultures in Modern Scandinavia (ca. 1750 – ca. 1920)* (De Gruyter, 2021) and *Nineteenth-Century Nationalisms and Emotions in the Baltic Sea Region: The Production of Loss* (Brill, 2021). She is currently working on a book on the Nordic emancipation novels of the 1850s.

Department of Linguistic, Literary and Aesthetic Studies – Nordic Literature
University of Bergen
anna.bohlin@uib.no

Alda Björk Valdimardóttir is a professor of comparative literature at the Icelandic and Comparative Cultural Studies faculty. She wrote her doctoral thesis on the novelist Jane Austen, emphazising contemporary popular women's writing.

Icelandic and Comparative Cultural Studies – Comparative Literature
University of Iceland
alda@hi.is

Sanna Schulte was born in Münster in 1985 and studied modern German literary history, German philology and political science at RWTH Aachen University. She received her doctorate with the dissertation on trauma and memory as a literary concept in Herta Müller's 'Reisende auf einem Bein' and 'Atemschaukel' and has taught and researched at the universities of Vienna and Graz as well as at the literature archive of the Austrian National Library. She is currently working on a habilitation-thesis on the subject of Nestbeschmutzung (nest soiling) as a Franz Werfel scholarship holder and is a substitute professor at the Chair of Heterogeneity Research at the TU Dortmund.

Heterogeneity Research
TU Dortmund University
sanna.schulte@tu-dortmund.de

Jacob Ølgaard Nyboe is associate professor of Danish at University of Iceland. He wrote his doctoral thesis on creative genre labels (genre signatures) in contemporary Danish literature. His most recent publications deals with neologisms in poetry and the work of Danish poet Marianne Larsen.

Faculty of Languages and Cultures – Danish Literature
University of Iceland
jacobon@hi.is